D1496105

A CATALOGUE OF THOMISTS, 1270-1900

A Catalogue of Thomists,
1270-1900

Leonard A. Kennedy, C.S.B.

Center for Thomistic Studies
University of St. Thomas
Houston, Texas 77006

Library of Congress Cataloging-in-Publication Data

Kennedy, Leonard A.
  A catalogue of Thomists, 1270–1900.

  Includes index.
  1. Thomists—Bibliography. 2. Thomists.
I. University of St. Thomas. Center for Thomistic
Studies. II. Title.
Z7128.S3K46   1987   [B839]   016.149   86-72913
ISBN 0-268-00763-2

Manufactured in the United States of America

To

Hugh Roy and Judith Marshall

and

Father Victor B. Brezik, C.S.B.

Co-Founders

of the

Center for Thomistic Studies

Contents

Introduction

The large and long-lived Thomist school of philosophy and theology has not yet been catalogued. Brief histories have been written to record the chief periods and representatives of the Thomist School, and many studies have been made of particular pockets of it. But these have not been all put together.

Certainly one reason for this not having been done is the enormity of the task. Indeed, a full account would require years of research, and result in a several-volume work. Since it was unlikely that anyone would attempt such a time-consuming and expensive enterprise, I have attempted something more modest. First, a decision was made to be tolerant of incomplete source material. Books not available in an excellent library, and difficult to obtain by inter-library loan, were not consulted unless they seemed likely to yield more than minimal new information. Second, it was decided to record only a minimum amount of information for each entry (this information is discussed below). Third, it was determined that entries would be made if some even of this minimal information were lacking, and even if it could sometimes have been obtained by lengthy research. A fourth decision was made to end the **Catalogue** at 1900. This was in the interests of size only. There have been so many Thomists in the present century, and their output has been so great, that including them would double the size of the **Catalogue.** Moreover, their names are readily available in V. J. Bourke's **Thomistic Bibliography, 1920-40** (St. Louis, 1945) and his **Thomistic Bibliography, 1940-78** (St. Louis, 1980).

Comments are in order concerning the material in the **Catalogue,** and its arrangement. It is readily seen that the Thomists are arranged first of all by century. Of course there is a problem concerning persons who died shortly after a century began: to what century do they belong? A stand has been taken in each case on an ad hoc basis.

Where numbers warrant, groupings have been made, within a century, by religious congregation, and by country. An attempt has been made also to identify popes and cardinals. Within each grouping, entries are arranged chronologically until 1800, after which an alphabetical arrangement has been made.

As concerns works written by Thomists, no effort has been made to be complete. If only one or two are mentioned in the sources, they are recorded. If many are mentioned, as is often the case, a selection has been made of what seemed to be the three or so most significant works, and printed works have been preferred. Moreover, the titles of works have been highly abbreviated in order to keep the **Catalogue** half as big as it would otherwise have been. It is important to realize, however, that at least one source has been listed for each entry in the **Catalogue**, and fuller information concerning works can be obtained from these sources. They are indicated by letters and numbers in square brackets; these refer to titles listed in **Works Referred To** (pp. 17-27). If works have been published, the place and date of first publication are shown in brackets, if these are known.

The most difficult problem has been: who was a Thomist? There are no criteria universally agreed on. The criteria used in this Catalogue are fairly liberal, such as an indication in the title of a work (**ad mentem Divi Thomae**) or the nature of a work (e.g., a commentary on Aquinas's **Summa theologiae**), or a statement of alleged Thomism by an author himself or one of his historians, unless this is contradicted by other evidence.

The **Catalogue** reveals a number of interesting aspects of the Thomist school. Let us indicate here the numbers of Dominicans, other religious, and non-religious, by century:

Century	Dominicans	Other Religious	Non-Religious	Total
13th	37	0	3	40
14th	73	4	20	97
15th	59	3	50	112
16th	142	36	38	216
17th	307	179	78	564
18th	166	50	33	249
19th	83	85	588	756
Totals	867	357	810	2034

If we accept the **Catalogue** as being an accurate reflection of the true situation, we see that more than half of the Thomists in each century were Dominicans, except for the nineteenth century, when only 11% were members of St. Thomas Aquinas's own community. Also, of other religious in the Thomist camp, only Jesuits have been present in large numbers, and their peak membership was in the seventeenth century.

There was a noticeable drop in the number of Thomists about 1400 A.D., but the number then increased until the eighteenth century, when a significant decrease occurred. In the nineteenth century the number of Thomists grew dramatically, though not among Dominicans. And this increase is explained only partially by the publication of **Aeterni Patris** in 1879, since there were many Thomists before that date. And we know that the twentieth century has witnessed an even greater growth in Thomist ranks, at least until 1960.

I would like to thank Sister Terese Auer, John Hood, Thomas Oey, James Witherspoon, and Karen Zedlick, for their assistance in preparing the **Catalogue.** Also Father Janusz Ihnatowicz for translating Polish source-material. Also the Pontifical Institute of Mediaeval Studies for the use of its library, and the Basilian Fathers of the Institute and of St. Michael's College, Toronto, who made life so pleasant outside the library. And Joanne Knasas for two years of revisions on the word-processor.

L. A. K.

Works Referred To

A   R. Aubert, **Aspects divers du néo-thomisme sous le pontificat de Léon XIII** (Rome, 1961).

A2   C. V. Andrade, Presencia del Tomismo en la Colombia del siglo XIX, **Tommaso d'Aquino nella storia del Pensiero** (Naples, 1974) II, 408-421.

B   A. Bacić, "Ex primordiis scholae thomisticae," **Angelicum** 4 (1927) 19-50, 224-251, 406-429.

B2   L. E. Boyle, "The **Summa Confessorum** of John of Freiburg...," **St. Thomas Aquinas, 1274-1974, Commemorative Studies** (Toronto, 1974) II, 245-268.

B3   E. Brocchieri, **Mons. Andrea Cappellazzi** (Vatican City, 1974).

B4   J. Bobik, **The Commentary of Conrad of Prussia on the De Ente et Essentia of St. Thomas Aquinas** (The Hague, 1974).

C   G. Cenacchi, **Tomismo e Neotomismo a Ferrara**
        (Vatican City, 1975).

C2   H. Cickowski, "Pologne," **Dictionnaire de
        théologie catholique** XII, 2, 2470-2515.

C3   R. Coulon, "Le mouvement thomiste au XVIIIe
        siècle," **Revue Thomiste** 19 (1911) 421-
        444.

C4   J. L. Perrier, "Un centre néo-thomiste en
        Colombe," **Revue Néo-Scolastique de
        Philosophie** 17 (1910) 256-260.

C5   P. Castagnoli, "Gli scolastici del secolo
        XIII e del principio del XIV," **Divus
        Thomas (Piacenza)** 30 (1927) 155-174.

C6   A. M. R."Cruz, Presencia de Santo Tomas de
        Aquino en las universidades
        hispanoamericanas: periodo hispanico,"
        **Tommaso d´Aquino nella storia del
        Pensiero** (Naples, 1974) II, 387-407.

C7   R. A. Couture, "Salmanticenses," **New Catholic
        Encyclopedia** (Washington, 1967) XII,
        987-988.

C8   F. J. Roensch, "Complutenses," **New Catholic
        Encyclopedia** (Washington, 1967) IV, 94-
        95.

D   P. Dezza, **Alle origini del Neotomismo** (Milan,
        1940).

D2   P. Dezza, **I Neotomisti Italiani del XIX
        secolo** (Milan, 1947).

E   W. P. Eckert, ed., **Thomas von Aquino:
        Interpretation und Rezeption** (Mainz,
        1974).

E2   M. S. Esturí, "El tomismo del Dr. José Forras
        y Bages, Obispo de Vich," **La Ciencia
        Tomista** 13 (1916) 271-284.

F   C. Fabro, **Breve Introduzione al Tomismo** (Rome
        etc., 1960).

F2   L. Foucher, **La philosophie catholique en
        France au XIXe siècle avant la
        renaissance thomiste et dans son report
        avec elle** (Paris, 1955).

F3   Dr. Ferreira-Deusdado, "La Philosophie
        thomiste en Portugal," **Revue Néo-
        Scolastique de Philosophie** 5 (1898) 305-
        325, 429-452.

G   J. E. Gurr, "Scholasticism," **New Catholic
        Encyclopedia** (Washington, 1967) XII,
        1158-1165.

G2   M. Grabmann, "De primitiva schola thomistica
      in Germania investigationes," **Xenia
      Thomistica** (Rome, 1925) III, 189-231.

G3   M. Grabmann, **Die Geschichte der katolischen
      Theologie seit dem Ausgang der Vaterzeit**
      (Freiburg, 1933).

G4   F. S. J. González, Santo Tomas de Aquino en
      Mexico, **Tommaso d´Aquino nella storia
      del Pensiero** (Naples, 1974) II, 422-424.

G5   O. Grundler, "The Influence of Thomas Aquinas
      upon the Theology of Girolamo Zanchi,"
      Studies in Medieval Culture, ed. J. R.
      Sommerfeldt (Kalamazoo, 1964) 102-117.

H   T. J. A. Hartley, **Thomistic Revival and the
      Modernist Era** (Toronto, 1971).

H2   V. Beltrán de Heredia, "La enseñanza de Santo
      Tomás en la Universidad de Alcalá," **La
      Ciencia Tomista** 13 (1916) 245-270.

H3   H. Hurter, **Nomenclator Literarius** (3rd ed.,
      Innsbruck, 1903-06).

J   R. Jacquin, "La philosophie de Saint Thomas
      d'Aquin en France au XIXème siècle,
      avant l'encyclique Aeterni Patris," **San
      Tommaso** (**Studi Tomistici** I; Vatican
      City, 1974) 325-337.

K   T. Kaeppeli, **Scriptores Ordinis Praedicatorum**
      (Rome, 1970-80).

K2   P. O. Kristeller, "Thomism and the Italian
      Thought of the Renaissance," **Medieval
      Aspects of Renaissance Learning** (Durham,
      N.C., 1974) 29-91.

K3   V. J. Koudelka, "S. Tommaso d'Aquino e la
      Boemia," **Tommaso d'Aquino nella storia
      del pensiero** (Naples, 1974) II, 348-353.

K4   L. A. Kennedy, "A Fifteenth-Century Authentic
      Thomist," **The Modern Schoolman** 42 (1965)
      193-197.

L   S. Swiezawskiego and J. Czerkawskiego, **Studia
      z Dzijów Myśle Swietego Tomasza z Akwinu**
      (Lublin, 1978).

L2   M. Lu, "La diffusione delle opere di Tommaso
      d'Aquino in Cina," **Tommaso d'Aquino
      nella storia del pensiero** (Naples, 1974)
      II, 367-374.

L3   G. M. Lohr, **Die Kolner Dominikanerschule vom 14. bis zum 16. Jahrhundert** (Frieburg i. S., 1946).

L4   F.-B. Lickteig, **The German Carmelites at the Medieval Universities** (Rome, 1981).

M   J. A. Mann, "Neo-Scholastic Philosophy in the United States of America in the Nineteenth Century," **Proceedings of the American Catholic Philosophical Association** (1959) 127-135.

M2   A. Michelitsch, **Kommentatoren zur Summa Theologiae des hl. Thomas von Aquin** (Graz and Vienna, 1924).

M3   M. Jugie, "Georges Scholarios et S. Thomas d´Aquin," **Mélanges Mandonnet** I, 422-440.

M4   G. M. Manser, **Das Wesen des Thomismus** (Freiburg i. S., 1935).

N   E. I. Narciso, **La Summa Philosophica di Salvatore Roselli et la Rinascità del Tomismo** (Rome, 1966).

N2   **New Catholic Encyclopedia** (Washington, 1967).

O   M. A. van den Oudenrijn, "Mechithar
        Sebastenus Thomista Orientalis,"
        Angelicum 8 (1931) 26-33.

O2   P. Orlando, "Napoli nella storia del
        neotomismo del secolo XIX," **Tommaso
        d´Aquino nella storia del pensiero**
        (Naples, 1974) II, 159-168.

O3   M. Van den Oudenrijn, "Une ancienne version
        arménienne de S. Thomas," **Mélanges
        Mandonnet** (Paris, 1930) I, 483-485.

P   A. Piolanti, **Pio IX e la rinascità del
        Tomismo** (Vatican City, 1974).

P2   S. Papadopoulos, **Hellenikai metaphraseis
        thomistikon ergon** (Athens, 1967).

P3   R. Palacz, "Le thomisme dans la philosophie
        Polonaise en la seconde moitiée du XVe
        siècle," **Tommaso d´Aquino nella storia
        del Pensiero** (Naples, 1974) II, 329-334.

P4   B. Peyrous, "Un grand centre de thomisme au
        XVIIe siècle...," **Divus Thomas
        (Piacenza)** 77 (1974) 452-473.

P5 A. Piolanti, **L´Accademia di Religione
        Cattolica** (Vatican City, 1977).

P6   A. Piolanti, **La lettera del Card. Lucido M. Parocchi sul Tomismo**, 1877 (Vatican City, 1985).

P7   A. Piolanti, **La Pontificia Accademia Theologica Romana** (Vatican City, 1982).

P8   A. Piolanti, **Il trattadello. . . di Fra Lorenzo da Bergamo O.P.** (Vatican City, 1974).

P9   A. Piolanti, "L'oratoriano Cesare Becilli (d. 1649) e lo studio della Summa Theologica di S. Tommaso," **Divinitas** 18 (1974) 180-189.

Q   J. Quétif and J. Echard, **Scriptores ordinis predicatorum**, I (to 1500) (Paris, 1719); II (1501 to 1720) (Paris, 1721); III (by Remigius Coulon, 1721 to 1740) (no place or date).

R   G. F. Rossi, **La filosofia nel Collegio Alberoni e il Neotomismo** (Piacenza, 1959).

R2   F. J. Roensch, **Early Thomist School** (Dubuque, 1964).

R3   G. Wallerand, "Henri Bate de Malines et S. Thomas d'Aquin," **Revue Néo-Scholastique de Philosophie** 36 (1934) 387-411.

R4   J. O. Riedl, **A Catalogue of Renaissance Philosophers** (Milwaukee, 1940).

R5   J. K. Ryan, "John Norris: A Seventeenth-century English Thomist," **The New Scholasticism** 14 (1940) 100-145.

R6   R. de Almeida Rolo, "Duas linhas de restauracâo tomista...," **Tommaso d'Aquino nella storia del Pensiero** (Naples, 1974) II, 230-241.

R7   G. de Rosa, "La figura dell'Angelico nel pensiero e nell'insegnamento teologico dell'Oriente cristiano slavo-bizantino," **Divus Thomas (Piacenza)** 52 (1949) 249-275.

R8   G. F. Rossi, **Il movimento neotomista piacentino. . .** (Vatican City, 1974).

R9   F. Russo, "La rinascità del tomismo in Calabria," **Aquinas** 8 (1965) 480-500.

S   I. C. Brady, "Scholasticism," **New Catholic Encyclopedia** (Washington, 1967) XII,

S2   S. Swiezawski, "Histoire de la pensée de S. Thomas: Recherches polonaises," **Tommaso d'Aquino nella storia del Pensiero** (Naples, 1974) II, 335-347.

S3   G. Sermoneta, "Per una storia del Tomismo hebraico," **Tommaso d'Aquino nella storia del pensiero** (Naples, 1974) II, 354-359.

S4   S. Swiezawski, "Le thomisme à la fin du moyen âge," **San Tommaso** (Studi Tomistici I; Vatican City, 1974) 225-248.

S5   C. Sommervogel, **Bibliothèque de la Compagnie de Jésus** (2nd ed., 1890-1932).

S6   J. L. Perrier, **The Revival of Scholastic Philosophy in the Nineteenth Century** (New York, 1909).

T   P. Mandonnet and J. Destrez, **Bibliographie Thomiste** (Le Saulchoir, 1921; Paris, 1960).

T2   A.-M. Viel, "Mouvement thomiste au dix-neuvième siècle," **Revue Thomiste** 17 (1909) 733-746; 18 (1910) 95-108.

T3   S. G. Papadapulos, "Thomas in Byzanz," **Theologie und Philosophie** 49 (1974) 274-304.

V   Vari autori, **Saggi sulla rinascità del
      Tomismo nel secolo** XIX (Vatican City,
      1974).

V2   C. Vansteenkiste, "Codici tomistici della
      biblioteca Domenicana di Vienna,"
      Angelicum 38 (1961) 133-165.

W   J. A. Weisheipl, "Thomism," **New Catholic
      Encyclopedia** (Washington, 1967) XIV,
      126-135.

W2   J. A. Weisheipl, "Scholasticism," **New
      Catholic Encyclopedia** (Washington, 1967)
      XII, 1165-1170.

W3   J. A. Weisheipl, **The Revival of Thomism: An
      Historical Survey** (no place, 1962).

W4   A. Walz, **Compendium Historiae Ordinis
      Praedicatorum** (Rome, 1948).

W5   A. Walz, "Il Tomismo dal 1800 al 1879,"
      Angelicum 20 (1948) 300-326.

Abbreviations

b.	born
Comm.	Commentary on
d.	died
De ente	Aquinas's **De ente et essentia**
ed.	edition
fl.	flourished
SCG	Aquinas's **Summa Contra Gentiles**
SCG I	The first book of SCG
ST	Aquinas's **Summa Theologiae**
I	The first part of ST
I-II	The first part of the second part of ST
II-II	The second part of the second part of ST

III   The third part of ST

Supplementum   The Supplement to III

Sent.   The **Sentences** of Peter Lombard

I Sent.   The first book of the **Sentences**

II Sent.   The second book of the **Sentences**

III Sent.   The third book of the **Sentences**

IV Sent.   The fourth book of the **Sentences**

* * * * *

These abbreviations should be understood as being in the appropriate grammatical case if they are found in latin titles.

THOMISTS

Thirteenth Century

DOMINICANS

England

Richard Knapwell (fl. 1288) [B K Q R2]
    Comm. I Sent.
    Contra corruptorem S. Thomae
        (Le Saulchoir, 1927)
    De unitate formae
    De immediata visione Dei

Robert Orphord (fl. 1292) [B Q R2 W]
    Contra dicta Henrici de Gandavo
    Contra dicta Aegidii Romani
    Correctorium

William de Hothum (1243?-98) [B Q R2]
    Commentarii in Sententiarum libros
    De immediata visione Dei
    De unitate formarum

Robert de Tortocollo (fl. 1300) [B]
    Correctorium corruptorii

Hugh of Manchester (fl. 1300) [K Q]
    Compendium theologiae
    Contra phanaticorum quorumdam deliria

William of Macclesfeld (d. 1303) [B Q R2]
    Contra Henricum de Gandavo
    Contra Corruptorem S. Thomae
    De unitate formarum
    Comm. Sent.

Thomas de Jorz (d. 1310) Cardinal [Q]
    Quodlibeta
    Comm. I Sent. (Venice, 1523)
    De visione beata

Thomas Sutton (d. 1315?) [B M2 Q R2 W]
    Completed Aquinas's Super Perihermenias et De
        generatione
    De unitate formarum (Rome, 1570-71)
    Quodlibeta
    De condordia librorum Thomae

                        France

Peter of Tarentasia (d. 1276) Cardinal [Q]
    Comm. Sent. (Toulouse, 1652)
    Quodlibeta
    De unitate formae

Peter of Conflans (d. 1290) [B]
    Epistola ad Kilwardby

Galienus de Orto (fl. 1290) [B2 K Q]
    Abbreviatio II-II
    Sermones

Bernard of Trille (1240?-92) [B Q R2]
    De cognitione animae conjunctae corpori
    De cognitione animae separatae (Toronto, 1965)
    De spiritualibus creaturis et de potentia Dei
    De differentia esse et essentiae

Raymond de Medullione (d. 1294) [B H3]

Hugh Aisselin of Billom (d. 1298) Cardinal [M2 Q]
    Super libros Sententiarum
    De unitate formarum
    De immediata visione divinae essentiae

William Bernardi (fl. 1298) [K Q]
    Translated some works of Aquinas into Greek

Bernard of Gannat (d. 1303) [M4]

Bernard of Auvergne (fl. 1303) [B K Q R2]
    Super libros Sententiarum (Lyons, 1519)
    Contra dicta Henrici de Gandavo

Giles of Lessines (1230?-1304?) [B]
    De unitate formae (Louvain, 1902)
    Comm. I, II, Sent.

John Quidort of Paris (d. 1306) [B G3 M2 Q R2]
    Comm. Sent.
    Quodlibeta
    De potestate regia et papali (Venice, 1506)
    Contra corruptorem Sancti Thomae
        (Cologne, 1516)
    De unitate formae

                        Germany

Conrad of Esslingen (fl. 1280) [K]
    Abbreviatio expositionis evangeliorum S. Thomae

Helvicus Teutonicus (fl. 1300) [K]
    De dilectione Dei et proximi (1485?)

                        Italy

Bombolognus of Bologna (fl. 1260) [B Q]
    Comm. Sent.

Nicholas Brunacci (fl. 1268) [B]

Hannibald de Hannibaldis (d. 1272) Cardinal [B K]
    Comm. Sent. (Basel, 1492)
    Quodlibeta

Baxianus of Lauda (fl. 1275) [K]
        Quaestiones XXXVI declarandae

James di Mercato (fl. 1277) [C5]

Reginald of Piperno (d. 1280) [Q]
    Completed ST III

Tommasello of Perugia (d. 1285) [B C5]
    Comm. I-III Sent.

Simon di Lentino (d. 1292) [C5]
    Quodlibeta

Latinus Malabranca of Rome (d. 1294) Cardinal [K]
    Planctus de morte Fr. Thomae (Munster, 1922)

John Balbus of Genoa (d. 1298) [B B2]
    Summa grammaticalis (seu Catholicon)
        (Mainz, 1450)
    De quaestionibus animae ad spiritum

Leonard de Pistoia (fl. 1300) [B]
    Speculum religionis christianae
    De praescientia et praedestinatione divina

Rambert dei Primadizzi of Bologna (d. 1308)
[B M2 Q]
    Apologeticum contra corruptorium S. Thomae

John of Gaiatia [B]

                         Scandinavia

Peter of Dacia (fl. 1270) [B]
    Acta Christinae Mirabilis Coloniensis

                           Spain

Ferrarius of Catalonia (fl. 1285) [G3]
    Quodlibet

Raymond Martini (d. 1290?) [B]
    Pugio fidei adversus Mauros et Iudaeos (1642)

                          OTHERS

Rabbi Hillel of Verona (fl. 1291) [S3]

Humbert of Preuilly (Cistercian) (d. 1298) [B]
    Comm. Sent.
    Comm. In Metaphysicam

Peter of Auvergne (d. 1304) [B G3 Q R2]
    Quaestiones super De caelo et mundo
    In parva naturalia (Padua, 1493)
    De motu animalium (Venice, 1566)
    In libros Metaphysicorum (Toronto, 1955)

Fourteenth Century

DOMINICANS

Armenia

Peter of Aragon [03]
    Translated III

James Thargmann [03]
    Translated III

Bohemia

Nicholas Biceps (fl. 1385) [K3]

Henry of Bitterfeld (d. 1405?) [K3 L]
    De vita activa et contemplativa

England

Conrad Ruffi (fl. 1319) [Q]
    Compendium expositionis S. Thomae in evangelia

Nicholas Trevet (1258?-1328?) [B W]
    Annales Plantaginistarum (London, 1845)
    Quodlibeta
    Quaestiones disputatae

John Bromyard (fl. 1340) [B2]
    Opus trivium
    Summa praedicantium

Thomas Waleys (d. 1350?) [W]
    Moralitates

Hugh de Lawthon (fl. 1350) [K]
    Comm. Sent.

Thomas of Claxton (d. 1415?) [W]
    Comm. Sent.
    Quodlibet

                    France and Switzerland

William of Paris (fl. 1310) [B2]
    De administratione sacramentorum

Guy of Evreux (fl. 1320) [B2]
    Regula mercatorum

James of Lausanne (d. 1321) [B]
    Comm. Sent.

Harvey Natalis (d. 1323) [B K Q R2 W]
    Comm. Sent. (Venice, 1505)
    Quodlibeta (Venice, 1486-1513)
    Tractatus octo (Venice, 1513)
    Defensio doctrinae Fr. Thomae

Nicholas de Freauvilla (1250-1323) Cardinal [B]

John Dominici of Montpellier (fl. 1324) [B K Q]
    Tabula super ST

Bernard Gui (1261?-1331) [B K Q]
    Legenda S. Thomae

Durandus of Aurillac (fl. 1334) [B K M2 Q]
    Scripta in IV Sententiarum libros
    Quodlibeta
    Liber contra Durandum

William Petri Godin (1260?-1336) Cardinal [B R]
    Lectura thomasina
    De principe et praelatorum potestate

Armand de Belvézer (d. 1340) [B K Q R2]
    Comm. De ente et essentia (Venice, 1472)
    Comm. I, III, Sent.
    Declaratio difficilium dictorum (Venice, 1477)

William of Cayeux (fl. 1340) [B2]
    Abridgement of Summa confessorum

Peter of La Palu (1275?-1342) Patriarch [B R W]
    Comm. Sent. (Venice, 1495)
    Quodlibeta
    Concordantiae ad Summam (Salamanca, 1552)

Bernard de Parentinis (d. 1342) [Q]
    Tractatus super missam
    Lilium (Paris, 1510)

Harvey de Cauda (fl. 1366) [B K Q]
    Tabula operum S. Thomae de Aquino
    Conclusiones in quibus S. Thomas videtur
        contradicere sibi ipsi

Elias Raimundi (fl. 1367) [Q]
    Litera encyclica ad universum ordinem
    De reliquiis S. Thomae in conventu Tolosano

Raymond Hugonis (fl. 1384) [K Q]
    Historia translationis corporis S. Thomae
        (Toulouse, 1693)

James of Metz [G2]
    Comm. Sent.

                        Germany

John Picardi of Lichtenberg (fl. 1311) [B]
    Comm. Sent.
    Quodlibeta

John of Freiburg (1250?-1314) [B2]
    Summa confessorum

John of Sterngassen (fl. 1314) [B]
    Comm. I Sent.
    Quaestiones quodlibetales

Berthold of Freiburg (fl. 1315) [B2]
    Summa confessorum germanice (printed)

Gerard of Sterngassen (fl. 1320) [B]
    Medulla languentis animae

H. Köflin (fl. 1320) [B K]
    Tabula super opera S. Thomae

Master Conrad (fl. 1323) [C5 G2]
    De intentionibus

Nicholas of Strasbourg (fl. 1325) [B]
    Sermones
    Summa philosophica

James Duèse of Cahors (1249-1334) Pope John XX [B]
    Redemptionem misit Dominus

Henry of Lübeck (d. 1336) [B]
    Quodlibeta

John of Bischofsdorf (fl. 1350) [K]
    Legenda B. Thomae

Henry Seuse (1295?-1366) [E]

Henry of Herford (d. 1370) [G2 G3]
    Catena entium

John of Dambach (d. 1377) [K3 Q W4]
    Consolatio theologiae

Henry de Cervo [G2 G3]
    Comm. Sent.

                    Italy

Guy Vernani of Rimini (fl. 1300) [K2]

Peter Calo (d. 1310) [B T]
    Vita S. Thomae (Toulouse, 1911)

Bencius of Alexandria (fl. 1310) [K]
    Relatio de canonizatione Thomae

Jordan di Rivalto (d. 1311) [C5]
    Sent.
    Sermones

Albert of Brescia (d. 1314) [B B2 G3 K Q]
    Commentarium in Sententias
    De officio sacerdotis

Peter de Andria (d. 1316) [B Q]
   De decem preceptis
   De vita spirituali

Remigio de Girolami (1235-1319) [B C E N Q W]
   Quaestiones theologicae
   Duo principia
   Sermones (Rome, 1901)

John Grimaldi (fl. 1319) [K]
   Super Physica
   Super De Anima

William of Tocco (d. 1323) [K Q T]
   Vita S. Thomae (Venice, 1588)

John of Parma (fl. 1324) [B]
   Defensio doctrinae thomisticae

Bernard Lombardi (fl. 1325) [B]
   Comm. Sent.

Peter Monticello of Cremona (d. 1327) [C]
   Comm. Philosophia Aristotelis

Bartholomew of Lucca (1245?-1327) [B Q]
   Historia ecclesiastica nova (Milan, 1727)
   Annales 1060-1303 (Florence, 1875)
   Hexaemeron (Siena, 1880)

Bartholomew de Abagliatis (d. 1329) [K Q]
   SCG translated into Armenian
   III translated into Armenian

Philip of Ferrara (fl. 1330) [C]
   Super dialecticam Petri Hispani
   Summa theologica catholicarum veritatum

Guy of Pila (d. 1331) [C]
   Summa theologica adversus haereses

Benedict de Asignano (fl. 1339) [K M2 Q]
   Quaestiones theologicae
   Concordantiae dictorum S. Thomae

Giles de Gallutiis of Bologna (d. 1340) [K]
   Summa casuum conscientiae

John of Aversa, Junior (fl. 1340) [K]
    Lectura psalterii

Gratiadei of Ascoli (d. 1341) [Q]
    In totam artem veterem Aristotelis
    Quaestiones super libros Physicorum
    Quaestiones in libros De anima
    Quaestiones theologicae et metaphysicae
        (Venice, 1484)
    Commentaria in Parva naturalia

Nicholas of Ascoli (fl. 1342) [K]
    Tabula II-II

Bartholomew of San Concordio (1263-1347) [B2 W]
    Compendium philosophiae moralis

John of Naples, I (d. 1350?) [B K Q]
    Comm. Sent.
    Quodlibeta XIII
    Quaestiones ordinariae (Naples, 1618)
    Sermones ad postulandam canonizationem
        Fr. Thomae

Andrew de Turri (fl. 1370) [K]
    Concordantiae locorum doctrinae S. Thomae

Aldobrandinus of Ferrara (fl. 1375) [C K Q]
    Officium translationis S. Thomae de Aquino

Thomasinus of Ferrara (fl. 1390) [Q]
    Scripta in IV libros Sententiarum
    Thomasina, seu compendium S. Thomae in
        I-III Sent.

Henry of Ferrara (fl. 1390) [C]

Thomas of Ferrara (fl. 1390) [C]
    Compendium librorum I-IV S. Thomae in
        Sententias

Dominic de Stelleopardis de Afragola (d. 1406) [K]
    Super De anima
    Compendium II-II

Poland

John Sartoris (fl. 1373) [K L S2]
    Itinerarium S. Thomae

Spain

Berengarius de Saltellis (fl. 1340) [K]
    Officium B. Thomae

AUGUSTINIANS

James Capocci of Viterbo (d. 1307) [B M4]
    Comm. Sent.
    Quodlibeta

Augustine Triumphus of Ancona (d. 1328) [M4]

BENEDICTINES

Ranulph Higden (fl. 1340) [B2]
    Speculum curatorum

Peter Roger (1291-1352) Pope Clement VI [B]
    Oratio panegyrica

OTHERS

Byzantium

Maximus Planudes (d. 1310) [M4 R7 T3]
    Translated into Greek Super symbolum
        apostolorum

Gregory Akindynos (fl. 1340) [M4]
    Translated SCG partly into Greek

Prochoros Kydones (1330?-69) [E M3 M4 T3]
   De esse et operatione (Paris, 1865)
   Translated into Greek De eternitate mundi

Demetrios Kydones (1324?-98) [E M M2 M3 M4 T3]
   Translated into Greek SCG, Opuscula
   Translated into Greek ST (Venice, 1750)

                         Elsewhere

John of Erfurt (Franciscan) (fl. 1305) [B2]
   Summa de poenitentia

Henry Bate of Mechelen (d. 1315?) [R3]
   Speculum divinorum (Louvain, 1931)

William of Pagula (fl. 1320) [B2]
   Oculus sacerdotis
   Summa summarum
   Speculum praelatorum

Conrad of Prussia (fl. 1323) [B4]
   Comm. De ente (The Hague, 1974)

Rabbi Judah ben David of Rome (1280?-1325) [S3]

Bartholomew of Capua (1284-1328) [B]
   Catalogus operum S. Thomae

Guy de Monte Rocherii (fl. 1330) [B2]
   Manipulus curatorum

John Baconthorpe (Carmelite) (1290?-1348) [W]
   Comm. Sent.
   Postill on St. Matthew
   Quaestiones canonicae

Raynerius of Pisa (d. 1351) [B2 W]
   Pantheologia

John de Burgo (fl. 1384) [B2]
   Pupilla oculi

Albericus of Rosate [B2]
   Repertorium iuris

John Corcoreci [O]
    Translated Aquinas's Comm. Sent. into Armenian

Lionardo of Perugia [G3]
    Quodlibeta

Paul Wlodkowic [L]
    Pisma Wybrane (Warsaw, 1968-69)

Philip of Bergamo [Q]
    Speculum regiminis

Philip of Pistoia [B C5]
    Correctorium corruptorii

Fifteenth Century

DOMINICANS

Bohemia

Augustine of Opavia [K]
  Super De ente

Byzantium

Manuel Calecas (d. 1410) [M3 R7 S4 T3]
  De fide (Paris, 1865)
  De ente et operatione (Paris, 1865)

France, Belgium, and Switzerland

Dominic of Flanders (d. 1422) [K]
  De celebratione festi S. Thomae

John Capreolus (d. 1444) [M2 Q]
  Defensiones theologiae Thomae (Venice, 1480-84)

William of Malliaco (d. 1462) [K Q]
  Tabulare S. Thomae

Lawrence Gervais (d. 1483) [K M2 Q V2]
  Copulata super totam Summam

Gil Charronnelle (fl. 1491) [R6]

Peter Piscatoris (d. 1508) [S4]

Germany, Austria, and Switzerland

John Herolt (d. 1418) [Q]
   Discipuli sermones

Amplonius Ratnynghen of Rheinbergen (fl. 1433)
[S4]

John of Soest (d. 1438) [G2 Q]
   Comm. Sent.

John Nider (1380?-1438) [G3 Q]
   Praeceptorium divinae legis (published)
   De contractibus (published)

Peter de Grussem (fl. 1438) [K]
   Sermo de S. Thoma

Henry Rotstock of Cologne (d. 1445) [K V2]
   De quo est et quod est

John Gotstich of Brandenburg (fl. 1450) [K]
   Sermones

Michael Tenteysen (fl. 1458) [K]
   De universali

Henry Kalt-Eysen (d. 1465) [Q]
   De universalibus
   Panegyris in laudem S. Thomae
   Tractatus de laudibus S. Thomae

Gerard of Elten (d. 1484) [K R4 W]
   Lectura super I

Caspar Grunewald (fl. 1490) [G3 M2 S4 W]
   Comm. ST

George Orter (fl. 1497) [Q]
   In conceptionem Deiparae Virginis
   Quadragesimale
   Sermones de tempore, per adventum, et de
      sanctis

Holland

Alan de Rupe (1428?-75) [K]
    De laudibus B. Thomae

Clement of Zoutelande (fl. 1485) [K]
    Conclusiones formales super I, I-II, III
        (Cologne, 1485)

Hungary

Leonard of Ragusa (d. 1480) [Q]
        Scholia in Summam

Peter Nigri (1435?-83) [Q W]
    Clypeus Thomistarum (Venice, 1481)

Nicholas de Mirabilibus (fl. 1500) [G3 W]
    De praedestinatione

Italy

John Dominic de Florentia (d. 1419) [K]
    Lectiones in Scripturam
    Sermones

Peter Lazari (fl. 1434) [K]
    Oratio ad honorem D. Thomae

James Arigonus (d. 1435) [M2 Q]
    Comm. I, I-II, III

John of Montenegro (d. 1444) [C]
    De conceptione B. Virginis
    Collationes cum Graecis

Bartholomew of Ferrara (1368-1448) [C]
    De Christo Jesu abscondito (Venice, 1555)

Saint Antoninus of Florence (1379-1459) [Q R4]
    Summa confessionalis (Rome, 1472)
    Summa theologiae moralis (Venice, 1477-79)

Simon de Florentia (fl. 1464) [Q]
  Historia S. Thomae

Leonard Matthaei of Udine (d. 1469) [K]
  Tabula super S. Thomam de philosophia
  Sermones

Giacomo of Ferrara (fl. 1470) [C]
  De Parvis naturalibus
  In De coelo et mundo
  In De anima

Théophile of Cremona (fl. 1471) [Q]
  Commentaria S. Thomae in Aristotelis libros
    (Venice, 1471)

John of Ferrara (fl. 1473) [C]

Conrad Mondonius of Asti (d. 1474) [K]
  Compilatio in I
  Quaestiones quodlibetales

Louis Longo (d. 1475) [M2 Q]
  Comm. I
  Commentaria in libros Physicorum

Leonard de Valle Brixiensi (d. 1478) [V2]
  Comm. I, III

Dominic of Flanders (d. 1479) [K Q]
  In libros Metaphysicae (Venice, 1496)
  Quaestiones in libros De anima (Venice, 1518)
  Summa divinae philosophiae

John Aquilano (d. 1479) [C]

Leonard Ser-Uberti (fl. 1481) [Q]
  De sacramento Corporis Christi

Peter of Bergamo (d. 1482) [K Q]
  Tabula aurea (Bologna, 1473)
  Concordantia locorum doctoris angelici in
    quibus sibi invicem adversari videntur
    (Venice, 1476)

John Gatto (1440-84) [C]

Philip de Barberiis (fl. 1490) [Q]
  De animorum immortalitate

Paul Barbus Soncinas (d. 1494) [C Q W]
    Epitoma Sententiarum a Capreolis disputatarum
        (Pavia, 1522)
    Super divina sapientia Aristotelis
        (Lyons, 1579)
    In libros Physicorum, et super artem veterem,
        Aristotelis

Peter of Vicenza (d. 1494) [Q]
    Opus aureum Angelici Doctoris

Louis of Ferrara (1453-96) [K Q]
    Aristotelis Politica (Rome, 1492)

Louis Valenza (d. 1496) [C]

Jerome Savonarola (d. 1498) [Q S4]
    Triumphum Crucis (Florence, 1497)
    De divisione, ordine, et utilitate scientiarum
        (Venice, 1522)
    Compendium totius philosophiae (Venice, 1542)

Vincent Bandello (1435-1506) [C K2]
    Quaestiones theologales
    Tabula Aurea

Francis Sicuro of Nardò [K2 S4]

                        Poland

Andrew Wanszyk (d. 1430) [K]
    Glossa S. Thomae super Mattheum

Matthias Hayn (d. 1476) [K]
    Super De ente
    Notabilia circa I-II
    Alphabetum ex dictis S. Thomae

                        Spain

Saint Vincent Ferrer (d. 1419) [Q S4]

Louis of Valladolid (d. 1436) [Q]
   Brevis historia de vita et doctrina Alberti
      Magni
   Historia de B. Thoma de Aquino
   Qualiter brachium B. Thomae fuit translatum
   Speculatio summa philosophiae

Gabriel Cassafages (fl. 1463) [Q]
     SCG in compendium redacta

John of Torquemada (1388-1468) Cardinal [K Q]
     Flores Sententiarum B. Thomae (Lyons, 1496)

Thomas of Toledo (fl. 1470) [Q]
     Super quodlibeta S. Thomae
     Super totam Summam theologicam

                        CARMELITES

Leonard de Remolt (fl. 1465) [L4]

John Beetz of Tienen (d. 1476) [L4]

Simon Carnificis de Oringa of Heilbronn (fl. 1492)
[L4]

                         OTHERS

                         Belgium

John Tinctor (d. 1469) [E V2 W]
   Comm. I

Denis the Carthusian (1402-71) [M2 R4 W]
   Compendium ST   (Venice, 1572)
   Comm. Sent.

                        Byzantium

Maximos Chrysoberges (fl. 1400) [T3]

Andrew Chrysoberges (d. 1451) [S4 T3]
    De divina essentia et operatione (1938)

Bessarion (1403-72) Cardinal [M4 T3]

John Argyropoulos (1415-87) [M4]
    Translated De Ente into Greek

                    England

John Mirfield (d. 1407) [B2]
    Florarium Bartholomaei

William Lyndwood (fl. 1420) [B2]
    Provinciale (Oxford, 1679)

Thomas Wygenhale (fl. 1450) [B2]
    Speculum iuratorum

                    France

John de Montesonos (d. 1412) [G3]

George de Rayn (fl. 1413) [M2]
    Excerpts from I-II and II-II

            Germany and Switzerland

Francis of Retz (d. 1427) [G3]
    Comm. Salve Regina

Henry Nolt (Franciscan) (d. 1474) [L3 S4]
    Comm. Sent.

Leonard of Brixental (d. 1478) [G3 W]

Gerard de Monte (d. 1480) [K Q W]
    Comm. De ente (Cologne, 1480?)
    Concordantia inter S. Thomam et Albertum
        (Cologne, 1480?)
    Decisionum S. Thomae concordantiae (Rome, 1934)

John Versor (d. 1485?) [R4 W]
   Comm. De ente
   Summulae Petri Hispani

John Nigri (d. 1489) [G3]
   Sermones

Henry de Belle of Löwenich (fl. 1490) [B2]

Lambert de Monte (d. 1499) [R4]

Cornelius Sneek [W]

John Stoppe [W]

                         Holland

Henry of Gorkum (1386-1431) [M2 R4 W]
   Compendium ST (Esslingen, 1473)
   Comm. Sent. (Basel, 1498)

                         Italy

Anthony Pizzamano (fl. 1490) [K2 S4 T W]
   Opuscula S. Thomae (Venice, 1490)
   Vita di S. Tommaso (Venice, 1508)

James Bruto (fl. 1496) [K4]
   Corona Aurea (Venice, 1496)

Anthony degli Agli [K2]

Dominic de´ Domenichi [K2]

Francis da Castiglione [K2]
   Vita S. Thomae

John Garzoni [K2]
   Vita S. Thomae

Lorenzo of Pisa [K2]

Poland

Paul of Worczyn (fl. 1424) [L]
    Super libros Ethicorum

Peter of Wichnian (fl. 1427) [L]
    Determinatio

John Heylin of Kamien (fl. 1480) [S4]

James of Gostynin (d. 1506) [C2 L P3]

John of Glogow (d. 1507) [C2 L S3]
    Comm. Metaphysica

Bartholomew of Jasto [S2]
    Comm. Sent.

James of Nowy-Sacaz [S2]
    Comm. Sent.

John of Slupcza [S2]
    Comm. Metaphysica

John Orient [S2]
    Comm. Metaphysica

John Taczel of Raciborz [S2]
    Comm. Sent.

Lawrence Grodziski of Poznan [S2]
    De Homine

Michael of Wroclaw [S2]
    De Homine

Nicholas Kozlowski [S2]
    Comm. Sent.

Pane of Worczyn [S2]
    Comm. in libros Ethicorum

Peregrinus of Opole [S2]

Peter Aurifaber of Cracow [S2]
    De Homine

Sigismund of Piyzdry [S2]
    Comm. Sent.

                        Scandanavia

Balthazar of Bingen [S4]

John Sartoris of Lingen [S4]

                        Spain

Joseph Albo (1380-1444) [S3]

Eli Xabilio (fl. 1475) [S3]

Sixteenth Century

DOMINICANS

Belgium

Peter Crockart of Brussels (d. 1514) [Q]
    In Aristotelis logicales libros (Paris, 1501)
    In De ente (Paris, 1509)
    Secunda secundae (Paris, 1512)

James of Brussels (fl. 1553) [M2 Q]
    Secunda secundae (Paris, 1515)

John Croocius (1479-1569?) [Q]
    Summa S. Thomae (Paris, 1520)

Balthazar Textor (1509-77) [M2 Q]
    Comm. II-II

James Faber (d. 1591) [M2 Q]
    Comm. III

Dalmatia

Augustine di Nale (d. 1527) [Q W4]
    Prima pars Summae (Venice, 1509)

France

Lambert Campester (fl. 1523) [Q]
    ST (Lyons, 1520)
    Catena aurea (Lyons, 1520)

William Totani (d. 1525) [Q]
    Questiones spiritualis convivii
        (Paris, 1508-10)

Vincent Theodorici (d. 1526) [Q]
    Tertia pars Summae (Paris, 1514)

John de Fenario (d. 1532) [Q]
    S. Thomae commentaria in Metheora
        (Venice, 1530)

John Nockart (fl. 1540) [Q]
    Commentarii Cajetani in primam partem
        (Paris, 1514)

John Viguerii (d. 1550) [Q]
    Institutiones ad scholasticam theologiam
        (Paris, 1553)

Claude of Spina (d. 1560) [Q]
    Epitome in Sententias (Paris, 1551)
    Commentaria in septem epistolas

Blase Foucher (d. 1588) [Q]
    Comm. I, III

                    Germany and Switzerland

Dietrich of Susteren (fl. 1509) [L3 Q]
    SCG (Cologne, 1499)
    Quaestiones disputatae (Cologne, 1499)

John de Werd (d. 1510) [E V2]
    Comm. SCG I
    Comm. De Ente

Ambrose Alemanus (d. 1515) [Q]
    Index incepta a Petro Bergomense, completa
        (Venice, 1497)

Conrad Koellin (d. 1536) [L3 Q R4]
    Comm. I-II (Cologne, 1512)
    Quodlibeta (Cologne, 1523)

Jerome Dungersheym Teutonicus (1465-1540)
[M2 Q R4]
    Compendium ST (Venice, 1585)

John Slotanus (fl. 1560) [Q]
    Postillae in epistolas et evangelia

Andrew Bodenstein [G4]
    Distinctiones thomistarum

                        Holland

Peter Fabri of Nijmegen (d. 1525) [Q]
    Tertia pars Summae (Paris, 1514)
    Cajetani commentaria in secundam secundae
        (Paris, 1519)

John Benedicti (1495?-1565) [Q]
    Introductiones dialecticae (Paris, 1538)

                        Italy

Dominic of Mortario (d. 1504) [Q]
    Index super volumina Capreoli

Thomas Donatus (d. 1505) [Q]
    Sermones
    Tractatus super ST

Simon Angelus de Rocci (1436-1508) [Q]
    Officium ecclesiasticum S. Ambrosii

Matthew Siculus (fl. 1509) [M2 Q]
    Prima pars Summae cum annotationibus
        (Venice, 1509)

Thomas Radinus (fl. 1511) [K2]
    Eulogium S. Thomae (Padua, 1511)

Gaspar of Perugia (fl. 1511) [Q]
    Sermones quadragesimales et dominicales
    Dichiarazione di S. Tommaso della confessione
        (Perugia, 1510)

Thomas of Calvisano (fl. 1512) [M2 Q]
    Comm. ST

Michael Saravetius (fl. 1517) [Q R4]
   De analogia entis contra Scotistas (Rome, 1515)
   De primis et secundis intentionibus
      (Rome, 1515)
   De principio individuationis (Rome, 1517)

John Louis Vivaldus (d. 1519) [Q]
   De pugna partis sensitivae et intellectivae
   Aureum opus de veritate contritionis
      (Saluzzo, 1503)

Zenobius Acciaioli (1462-1520) [Q]
   Justinus philosophus martyr latine redditus
   Aristotelis Ethica Nicomachea (Florence, 1504)

Cornelius Sambucus (fl. 1520) [Q]
   Scripta S. Thomae in Sententias
      (Venice, 1519-20)

J. Cremonensis (fl. 1520) [Q]
   Revocatio Martini Lutherii Augustiniani
      (Cremona, 1520)

Angelus of Savigliano (fl. 1521) [Q]
   SCG (Lyons, 1521)

Silvester Mazzolini de Prierio (1460-1523)
[B2 M2 Q R4]
   Epitoma Capreoli (Cremona, 1497)
   Malleum contra Scostistas (Bologna, 1514)
   Conflatum ex S. Thoma (Perugia, 1519)

Sebastian of Perugia (1445?-1525) [Q]
   Vita Beatae Columbae (Bologna, 1521)

Francis Silvester (1474?-1525) [Q]
   In libros Posteriorum Aristotelis et S. Thomae
      (Venice, 1517)
   In SCG commentaria (Paris, 1552)

Jerome of Monopoli (d. 1528) [Q]
   Commentaria in libros Metaphysicorum

Paul Butigella (fl. 1530) [M2 Q]
   Comm. II-II, III

Jerome Balbus (fl. 1530) [Q]
   De civili et bellica fortitudine (Rome, 1526)

John Faber (d. 1530) [Q]
    Oratio funebris Maximiliani Augustae (1519)

Jerome Fantonus (1462-1532) [C Q]
    Index in volumina Capreoli
    Tabula super opera Scoti pro schola Aquinatis
      (Venice,1588)

Thomas de Vio Cajetanus (1469-1534) Cardinal [M2 Q]
    Comm. ST (Lyons, 1540-41)
    In De ente (Lyons, 1541)

Chrysostom Javellus (fl. 1538) [M2 Q W]
    Totius philosophiae compendium (Venice, 1536)
    Questiones super Metaphysices (Venice, 1564)
    Comm. I (Mainz, 1611)

Vincent Giachanus (or Giacharus) (fl. 1540) [Q]
    Opera moralia (Venice, 1538)
    Tabula aurea (Rome, 1539)

Anthony Beccaria (d. 1543) [C M2 Q]
    Comm. I, I-II, II-II
    Commentaria in Metaphysicam, Physicam, etc.

Albert Paschaleus (d. 1544) [Q]
    De optimo philosophorum genere (Venice, 1532)

John Francis Beatus (fl. 1545) [Q]
    In secundum Physicorum

Paul Manna (fl. 1545) [M2 Q]
    Comm. ST
    In universam philosophiam

Paul of Cremona (fl. 1545) [C]
    Comm. ST
    Comm. Opera Aristotelis

Bartholomew Spina (d. 1546) [Q]
    Metaphysicarum digressionum S. Thomae
      defensiones (Venice, 1517)
    Propugnaculum Aristotelis de immortalitate
      animae (Venice, 1519)
    De immortalitate animae (Venice, 1519)

Thomas Badia (d. 1547) [C]
    De immortalitate animae
    De analogia entis
    Quaestiones metaphysicae

John Chrysostom of Bagnuolo (fl. 1547) [M2 Q]
    Comm. I, III

Jerome Papinus of Lodi (fl. 1548) [M2 Q]
    Comm. ST
    Opuscula philosophica ad mentem S. Doctoris

Francis Romeo (d. 1552) [H3 W]
    De libertate operum (Lyons, 1538)

Ambrose Catharinus (1487-1553) [Q]
    Annotationes de commentariis Cajetani
        (Paris, 1535)
    Disceptationes ad Dominicum de Soto
        (Rome, 1551)
    Tractatus theologici plures (Rome, 1551-52)

Lawrence of Bergamo (d. 1554) [P8]
    Trattadello (Vatican City, 1974)

Peter Bertanus (1501-58) Cardinal [M2 Q3 W4]
    Comm. ST

Thomas Stella (d. 1566) [W]
    Trattato sulla carita
    Sermoni

Thomas Neri (d. 1568) [Q3]
    Scriptum S. Thomae in secundum Sententiarum

James Naclantus (d. 1569) [Q3 W]
    De jure divino ex sententia D. Thomae
        (Venice, 1557)
    Theoremata metaphysica (Venice, 1557)
    Theoremata naturalia (Venice, 1557)

Thomas Casellius (fl. 1571) [Q3]
    De conceptione B. Virginis

Antonio Ghislieri (1504-72) Pope Pius V [B3]
    Mirabilis Deus (Rome, 1567)

Adrian Valenticus (fl. 1572) [Q3]
   De inquirendis puniendisque haereticis (Venice,
   1542)

Vincent Patinas (d. 1575) [Q3]
   Dilucidationes librorum De anima, necnon
      commentariorum Aquinatis (Bologna, 1575)
   Commentaria in libros Posteriorum et
      Metaphysicorum

Angelus de Sestro (d. 1580) [Q]
   Annotationes super Praedicabilia,
      Praedicamenta, Physicam, et Metaphysicam
   Questiones de angelis
   In De ente

Remigius Nanni (1530?-80) [Q]
   Opuscula (Venice, 1562)

John Bartholomew Ferrus of Lugo (fl. 1581) [Q]
   Oratio in laudem S. Thomae

Paul Costabili (d. 1582) [C]

Jerome Vielmius (1519-83) [M2 N Q T W4]
   De D. Thomae doctrina et scriptis (Padua, 1564)
   Commentaria in Summam et in Epistolam ad
      Romanos

Giles of Bologna (fl. 1584) [Q]
   Opera theologica et philosophica

Thomas Peregrinus (fl. 1584) [Q]
   Commentaria super Metaphysicam
   In Physicam commentaria

Francis Goraceus (d. 1585) [M2 Q]
   Collatio hominis lapsi ad statum naturae
      integrae
   Comm. I-II, II-II

Paulinus Berardini (1515?-85) [Q]
   Tabula in commentariis Cajetani super
      Summam D. Thomae

Vincent Herculanus (1516-86) [Q]
   Sententiae praedicabiles
   Commentaria in Dialecticam Petri Hispani

Hippolytus Mary Becaria (fl. 1589) [Q]
    Comm. I, I-II
    In libros Physicorum
    In De anima

Seraphinus de Vannis (fl. 1589) [Q]
    Oratio in festo S. Thomae

Bartholomew a Martyribus (1514-90) [M2 W]
    Comm. I-II (Venice, 1580)
    Comm. III (Venice, 1582)

Modestus of Vicenza (fl. 1590) [M2 Q]
    Comm. III

Matthias Aquarius (fl. 1591) [M2 Q]
    Controversiae inter D. Thomam et ceteros
        theologos ac philosophos (Venice, 1589)
    Formalitates juxta doctrinam D. Thomae
        (Naples, 1605)

Clement Giffonellus (d. 1593) [Q]
    Apologeticum questionum de praedicatione
        naturali

John Ambrose Barbavara (d. 1594) [M2 Q]
    Comm. I
    Oratio in laudem D. Thomae (Venice, 1548)

Gabriel Alessandri (d. 1595) [Q]
    De Domini resurrectione (Milan, 1588)

George Busti (1500-96) [Q]
    Quaestiones philosophicae et theologicae
        (Venice, 1574)

Eustachius Dalei (fl. 1600) [Q]
    Index in opera omnia Cajetani, non perfectus
    In De anima

Stephen Guaraldus of Cento (fl. 1600) [Q]
    Commentaria Conradi Koellin in Primam Secundae
        (Venice, 1589)

Seraphinus Maio (fl. 1605) [Q]
    Stimulus theologorum super partem primam
    Oratio in laudem S. Thomae (Naples,1605)

Matthias Fasano da Ottato (d. 1607) [Q]
    Vita dell'angelico dottore (Venice, 1607)

Paul Grysaldus (d. 1609) [M2 Q]
    Enchiridion totius Summae D. Thomae
    Tractatus de angelis

Thomas Buoninsegni (d. 1609) [Q]
    Questiones disputatae S. Thomae (Venice, 1588)
    Utrum principium individuationis sit materia
    De motoribus corporum coelestium

Vincent Giaccari [W4]
    Re-edited Tabula aurea

Bartholomew Marzolus [R4]
    Dubium super logicam Pauli Veneti

Vincent Septartius [M2 Q]
    Comm. III

Francis Taegius [R4]
    Comm. S. Thomae De fallaciis

                         New World

Anthony de Hinojosa [G4]

Bartholomew of Ledesma [C6]
    De septem sacramentis (Mexico City, 1556)

Joseph Calderón [G4]

Peter de la Peña [C6]
    Comm. I

Thomas de Mercado [G4]

                          Poland

Camillus Samboriensis (1575?-1605) [Q]
    Commentaria in Aristotelem et S. Thomam

Portugal

Francis Dorta (fl. 1560) [M2 Q]
    Comm. ST

Jerome Oleaster (d. 1563) [H3 W]

Anthony of St. Dominic (fl. 1579) [M2 Q]
    Notae in omnes partes Summae

Thomas de Penha (fl. 1580) [Q]
    Officium de S. Thoma

Francis Foreiro (1510?-81) [W]
    Scriptural Commentaries
    Meditations

Anthony Senensis (fl. 1585) [M2 Q R4 T]
    Testimonia Patrum et quaecumque citat S. Thoma
        (Antwerp, 1569)
    Catena aurea (Antwerp, 1573)
    Commentarius in Genesim (Antwerp, 1573)

Spain

Angelus Estanyol (fl. 1507) [Q]
    Opera logicalia secundum viam S. Thomae
        (Barcelona, 1504)

Michael de Olosabal (fl. 1515) [Q]
    Commentarius Cajetani in primam secundae
        (Paris)

Matthias de Paz (fl. 1517) [M2 Q]
    Comm. ST

Dominic de Mendoza (fl. 1518) [Q]
    Quaedam theologica

Diego de Deza (1444-1523) [M2 Q S4]
    Defensorium S. Thomae (Seville, 1491)

John Hurtado de Mendoza (fl. 1525) [Q]
    Comm. I-II

Paul of Leon (fl. 1528) [Q]
    Guia del cielo (Salamanca, 1553)

John de Villerio (fl. 1531) [Q]
    Summa S. Thomae (Paris, 1520)

Francis of Vitoria (1480?-1546) [M2 Q W]
    Comm. III (Vergard, 1904)
    Comm. II-II (Salamanca, 1932-52)

Bernard de Nieva (fl. 1556) [Q]
    Summario manual de la Christiana conciencia
        (Medina del Campo, 1556)

Alphonse of Herrera (d. 1558) [Q]
    De valore bonorum operum (Paris, 1540)

Dominic de Soto (1494-1560) [M2 Q]
    Comm. I, II
    De iustitia et iure (Salamanca, 1556)

Melchor Cano (1505?-60) [M2 Q]
    Comm. I
    Comm. I-II (Salamanca, 1503)
    De locis theologicis (Salamanca, 1563)

Ambrose de Salazar (1522-60) [M2 Q]
    Comm. I

Peter de Soto (d. 1563) [Q]
    Institutiones christianae (Antwerp, 1551)

Peter de Sotomayor (d. 1564) [M2]
    Comm. I, I-II

John de la Peña (d. 1565) [M2 Q]
    Comm. I, III

John de Ochoa (d. 1565) [Q]
    Conclusiones Summae in carmen redactae
        (Rome, 1565)

Thomas Manrique (d. 1573) [Q]
    D. Thomae opera (Rome, 1570)
    Tractatus in Summam

Bartholomew de Carranza (1503?-76) [G3 W]
    Summa conciliorum (Venice, 1546)

Mancio de Corpore Christi (1509?-76?) [M2 Q]
    In S. Thomae Summam, eiusque interpretem
        Cajetanum

John Gallo (d. 1577) [Q]
    Oratio in laudem S. Thomae (Louvain, 1567)
    Commentarium in quartum Sententiarum

Bernard de Albuquerque (1489?-1579) [Q]
    Catechismus de doctrina christiana

Bartholomew of Medina (1527-81) [M2 Q]
    Comm. I-II (Salamanca, 1577)
    Comm. III (Salamanca, 1578)

Francis Garcia (d. 1583) [Q W4]
    Emendatio erratorum in Summa (Tarragona, 1578)

Martin of Ledesma (1510?-84) [M2 Q]
    Commentaria in quartum Sententiarum
        (Coimbra, 1555-60)
    Comm. III

Francis de Sancta Cruz (fl. 1591) [M2 Q]
    Comm. I

John Vincente (d. 1595) [M2 Q]
    Comm. I-II (Rome, 1591)

Alphonse de Luna (1553?-97) [Q]
    Observationes ad tertiam partem
        (Salamanca, 1597)

Dominic Bañez (1528-1604) [M2 Q]
    Comm. I, II-II (Salamanca, 1584)
    Comm. III

Gaspar of Corduba (fl. 1604) [Q]
    De poenitentia
    De visione, scientia, et nominibus Dei

Didacus Yangas (d. 1606) [Q]
    Scholia in D. Thomam

Didacus Mas (1552?-1608) [M2 Q]
    Comm. III
    De ente et eius proprietatibus (Valencia, 1578)

Sebastian Bravo (d. 1608) [Q]
    Collectanea aurea sacrae scripturae
        (Complutum, 1595)

AUGUSTINIANS

Alonso de la Vera Cruz (fl. 1535) [C6 G4]
    Recognitio summularum

Francis of Christ (d. 1587) [G3]

Augustine de SS. Trinitate (d. 1589) [M2]

Peter of Aragon (d. 1592) [M2]
    Comm. II-II (Salamanca, 1584)
    Comm. III (Venice, 1600)

CARMELITES

John Wyrich of Neuss (1441?-1515) [L4]

Peter Wirt of Heilbronn (d. 1517) [L4]

Henry Seytz (d. 1531) [L4]

Henry Benedictus (fl. 1590) [M2]
    Comm. I

Benedict Henricus (fl. 1590) [M2]
    Comm. I-II

JESUITS

Claude le Jay (1504-52) [W]

Saint Francis Borgia (d. 1572) [M2]
    Praecipuae divi Thomae materiae
        (Valencia, 1550)

Didacus Ledesma (1519-75) [M2]
    Tabella brevis ST (1651)

Augustine Agostini (d. 1583) [M2]
    Comm. I

John Maldonato (d. 1583) [P9]
    Comm. I-II
    De gratia

Th. Peltanus (d. 1584) [M2]
    Comm. I

J. Bleuse (fl. 1584) [M2]
    Comm. III

Laurinius (fl. 1587) [M2]
    Comm. I-II

J. Castelarius (fl. 1589) [M2]
    Comm. I

Augustine Giustiniani (d. 1590) [M2]
    Comm. I (Rome, 1583)

G. Serrao (fl. 1590) [M2]
    Comm. I-II

Fr. Bonaventura (fl. 1592) [M2]
    Comm. II-II

Mutius de Angelis (fl. 1591-94) [M2]
    Comm. I, II

Francis of Toledo (1532-96) Cardinal [M2 T]
    Comm. in libros De physica (Venice, 1573)
    Comm. ST (Rome, 1869-70)

James Tyrie (1543-97) [M2]
    Comm. ST

Anthony Carvalho (1541-1601) [M2]
    Comm. I-II, II-II

Peter Luiz (1539-1602) [M2]
    Comm. I, III

Michael Marcos (1542-1602?) [M2]
    Comm. II-II

Gregory of Valencia (1551-1603) [M2]
    Comm. ST (Ingolstadt, 1591-97)

John Azor (d. 1603) [M2]
    Comm. ST
    Institutiones morales (Rome, 1600-11)

Gabriel Vasquez (1551-1604) [M2]
    Comm. ST (Complutum, 1598-1615)

Christopher Gil (1555-1608) [M2]
    Comm. I (Lyons, 1610)
    Comm. III

Peter de Arrubal (1559-1608) [M2]
    Comm. I (Madrid, 1619-22)

John Leo of Jerez (1540-1609) [M2]
    Comm. I, III

Benedict Pereyra (1535?-1610) [M2]
    Comm. I, III
    Physics (Rome, 1562)

Anthony Arias [G4]
    Compendium commentariorum Toleti

Peter Sanchez [G4]

OTHERS

Belgium

Augustine Hunnaeus of Mechelen (1522-87) [R4]
    Totius Summae conclusiones (printed)

John Clarius (fl. 1596) [M2]
    Comm. I

John Anthony of Pelta (d. 1606) [M2]
    Comm. I

France

Alphonse Carilius (fl. 1582) [M2]
    Comm. III

Berardus Bongean (1538-1607) Cardinal [M2 R4]
    Epitome in ST (Venice, 1564)

Richard Flaminius [M2]
    Comm. III

Germany

Martin Pollich (d. 1513) [R4]
    Comm. Thomist logic

Leonard Holzer (fl. 1573) [M2]
    Comm. I

Girolamo Zanchi (1516-90) [G5]
    On the Trinity (Geneva, 1619)
    On Creation (Geneva, 1619)
    On Redemption (Geneva, 1619)

Henry Altensteig [M2]
    Index in Thomam et alios scolasticas

Erasmus Wonsidel [R4]
    Comm. Thomist logic

Greece

Rabbi Joseph Taitazàq (fl. 1525) [S3]

Italy

Obadiah Sforno (1470?-1550?) [S3]

Anthony Pantusa (d. 1562) [R9]
    Liber de praedestinatione (Rome, 1545)
    Quaestiones theologicae (Venice, 1596)

Ricasoli (d. 1570) [M2]
    Comm. I-II, III

Hyppolitus Zaffaleoni (Servite) (d. 1575) [C]
    Tractatus philosophicus

Pius Bentivoglio (fl. 1585) [M2]
    Compendium theologiae D. Thomae (Venice, 1585)

Louis Carboni (d. 1597) [M2 R4]
    Compendium ST (Venice, 1587)

Caesar Baronius (1538-1607) Cardinal [M2]
    Comm. I-II (Rome, 1759)

Jehi´él of Pisa [S3]

Joseph Abrabanel [S3]

Judah Abrabanel [S3]

Paul Pacelli [K2]
    Eulogia S. Thomae

Paul Ragio [T]
    La vita dell´Angelico (Naples, 1580)

Peter Aretino [T]
    La vita di San Tommaso (Venice, 1543)

                        New World

Domiâo da Costa (d. 1563) [F3]

Francis Naranjo [G4]

Peter Ortigosa [G4]

Anthony Rubio [G4]
    Logica Mexicana

                        Poland

Matthias Valerian of Warsaw (fl. 1550) [L]
    Concio de D. Thoma

Michael Folkener of Wroclaw [P3 S2]
    Epitome figurarum (Cracow, 1518)
    Quaestiones quodlibetales

Stanislas Biel [S2]
    Comm. II-II

Spain

Jerome Perez (Mercedarian) (fl. 1548) [M2]
   Comm. I, I-II (Madrid, 1548)

Bartholomew Torres (d. 1568) [M2]
   Comm. I (Complutum, 1567)

Melchior Lobat (fl. 1577) [M2]
   Comm. I

Sebastian Perez (fl. 1588) [M2]
   Comm. I-II

John Mingues (fl. 1592) [M2]
   Compago artificiosa ST (Valencia, 1592)

Unknown Country

Vincent Dodi [Q]
   Apologia pro doctrina S. Thomae

Seventeenth Century

DOMINICANS

Belgium

Peter of Lorca (d. 1612) [H2]
    Comm. II-II (Alcala, 1609-16)

Philip Wannemakerus (1586-1630) [Q]
    Oratio panegyrica in S. Thomam
        (Ypern, Belgium, 1620)

Adrian a Cruce (d. 1634) [Q]
    Oratio in laudem S. Thomae (Artois, 1614)

Nicholas Jansenius (d. 1634) [Q]
    Panegyricus D. Thomae (Louvain, 1621)
    In apologiam Duns Scoti (Cologne, 1622)

Peter le Clerc (d. 1636) [Q]
    Oratio in laudem S. Thomae (Lille, 1629)

Hyacinth Husselius (1587-1638) [M2 Q]
    Comm. ST

Peter du Fay (1585-1639) [Q]
    De poenitentia (Douai, 1626)

Francis Capronius (1586-1642) [M2 Q]
    Comm. ST

Francis Hyacinth Choquetius (d. 1645) [Q]
    Laudatio D. Thomae (Douai, 1618)

Andrew Willart (1575-1648) [Q]
    Le glorieux triomphe de S. Thomas

Louis Bertrand Loth (d. 1652) [Q]
   Philosophia ad mentem S. Thomae
   Super universam Summam

Francis Vermeil (1597?-1657) [Q]
   Comm. I (Douai, 1650)

Alexander Sebille (1612?-57) [M2 Q]
   Resolutiones secundum doctrinam D. Angelici
   Comm. I
   Augustini et Patrum interpres thomisticus
      (Mainz, 1652)

Vincent Willart (d. 1658) [Q]
   S. Thomae sententia (Mund, Switzerland, 1645)
   Expositio in regulam B. Augustini (Mund, 1645)
   Les fruits de l'oraison (Mund, 1645)

Francis Deurwerders (1616?-66) [Q]
   Militia angelica D. Thomae (Louvain, 1659)

John Baptist Verjuys (fl. 1667) [M2 Q]
   Comm. ST

Thomas Leonardi (1596-1668) [Q]
   De prima hominis institutione (Brussels, 1661)

William Seguier (1600-71) [M2]
   Triumphus doctrinae S. Thomae
   Comm. I-II
   Vita S. Thomae

John Baptist Wouters (fl. 1684) [Q]
   Vita S. Thomae

John Anthony D'Aubermont (1612-86) [Q]
   Oratio in S. Thomam (Louvain, 1650)
   D. Thomae Contra impugnantes Dei cultum
      (Louvain, 1676)

Paul Fasseau (d. 1691) [Q]
   De praemotione physica (Douai, 1670)

Henry Collins (fl. 1692) [Q]
   Theses de gratia (Louvain, 1692)

Louis Bertha (1620-97) [Q]
   Misericors sponsus (Antwerp, 1665)

Charles Petri (1623-1703) [Q]
    Conciones thomisticae (Antwerp, 1693)
    Discursus morales (Cologne, 1698)

Francis Joyeulx (1644-1707) [Q]
    Theologia (Louvain, 1680)
    Theses theologicae (Louvain, 1683-92)

                        Bohemia

Thomas Elias Willinger (d. 1703) [K3 Q]
    Tractatus de iure et iustitia (Prague, 1692)

Thomas Albert Tranquillo (1648-1707) [Q]
    Theses ex universa philosophia
        (Old Prague, 1682)
    Conclusiones theologicae (Old Prague, 1690)
    Assertiones ex universa philosophia
        (Old Prague, 1693)

Augustine Adler (1643-1711) [K3 Q]
    Commentaria in Aristotelis logicam
    Logica

Ambrose Peretius (1671-1712) [Q]
    Commentaria in Aristotelis logicam

                        France

Reginald Chauvanac (d. 1618) [Q]
    Meditationes de S. Thoma

Nicholas Coeffeteau (1574-1624) [Q]
    Essai des questions théologiques (Paris, 1607)

Peter Girardel (1575?-1633) [Q]
    Comm. ST

John Testefort (1575-1644) [Q]
    Philosophiae thomisticae pars prima (Lyons, 1634)
    Le chemin de la perfection

Dominic Dunant (1593?-1646) [Q T]
    Vie de S. Thomas d´Aquin (Toulouse, 1628)

John Senarensis (d. 1653) [Q]
   Meditations de S. Thomas (Toulouse, 1683)

Nicholas le Febre (1588-1653) [Q]
   Doctrinae Athanasii Alexandri (Paris, 1631)

Andrew Widehen (d. 1654) [Q]
   De gratia

Peter Jammy (d. 1663) [Q]
   Veritates de auxilio gratiae
      (Grenoble, 1658-59)

Bernard La Palisse (d. 1666) [M2 Q]
   Comm. III

Peter du Four (1597?-1670) [Q]
   Quaestiones de gratia efficaci

Peter Labat (d. 1670) [M2 Q]
   Theologia scholastica (Toulouse, 1658-61)

Peter Pelican (1592-1673) [Q]
   S. Thomae opuscula (Paris, 1656)

John Nicolai (1594-1673) [G3 Q T W4]
   De gratia divina (Paris, 1656)
   Summa theologica (Paris, 1663)
   In Catenam auream praefatio (Paris, 1668)

Simon Roger (1597?-1673) [Q]
   Le Seneque expliqué (Rouen, 1651)

Bernard Guyard (1601-74) [M2 Q]
   Discrimina inter doctrinam Thomisticam et
      Jansenianam (Paris, 1655)
   Utrum S. Thomas calluerit linguam graecam
      (Paris, 1667)

Vincent Baron (1604-74) [M2 Q]
   Theologia moralis (Paris, 1665)
   SS. Augustini et Thomae mens de libertate
      humana (Paris, 1666)
   Theologiae moralis summa (Paris, 1667)

Vincent de Contenson (1641-74) [Q]
   Theologia mentis et cordis (Lyons, 1673-75)

Anthony Reginaldus (1605-76) [M2 Q T]
    Quaestio de vera intelligentia (Paris, 1638)
    D. Thomae tria principia (Toulouse, 1679)
    Circa gratiam (Antwerp, 1706)

Francis Combefis (1605-79) [Q]
    In editionem novam Catenae aureae (Paris, 1668)
    Discussiones ad prolusionem (Paris, 1668)

Francis Felix (fl. 1680) [Q]
    Totius doctrinae philosophicae tractatio
        (Grenoble, 1669)

John Baptist Gonet (1616-81) [M2 Q]
    De moralitate actuum humanorum (Bordeaux, 1664)
    Clypeus theologiae thomisticae
        (Bordeaux, 1659-69)
    Manuale Thomistarum (Béziers, 1680)

Hyacinth Chalvet (1605-83) [M2 Q]
    Theologus Ecclesiastes (1653-82)

Nicolaus Arnu (1629-84) [Q]
    Clypeus philosophiae thomisticae
        (Béziers, 1672)
    Comm. I (Rome 1679, Padua 1691)

Louis Bancel (1628?-85) [Q]
    Moralis D. Thomae (Avignon, 1677)
    Brevis universae theologiae cursus
        (Avignon, 1684-92)
    De militia angelica S. Thomae

Mark Douferre (1627?-86) [Q]
    Idea perfecti sacrae theologiae doctoris
        (Caen, 1682)

René Malapert (fl. 1687) [M2]
    Comm. III

David Lenfant (1603-88) [M2 Q]
    S. Thomae Biblia (Paris, 1657-59)

John Charles Ducos (1627?-92) [Q]
    Le pasteur apostolique (Toulouse, 1697)

Raymond Mailhat (1611-93) [Q]
    Summa philosophiae (Toulouse, 1652)

Oliver Fournier (1628-94) [M2 Q]
    Comm. I, I-II, III

Anthony Goudin (1639-95) [N Q]
    Philosophia (Milan, 1675)

James Quétif (1618-98) [Q]
    Hieronymi de Medicis explicatio Summae
        (Paris, 1657)

Charles Bouquin (1622-98) [Q]
    Solis Aquinatis splendores (Lyons, 1677)

Francis Penon (1623-99) [M2 Q]
    Summae rhythmica synopsis (Paris, 1651)

Anthony Du Prat-Chassagny (1628-1703) [Q]
    La morale du Docteur Angelique (Lyons, 1690)

James-Casimir Guerinois (1640-1703) [N Q S6]
    Clypeus philosophiae thomisticae (Venice, 1716)

James Maison (1617-1704) [Q]
    Compendaria theologiae moralis explicatio
        (Paris, 1676)

Anthony Massoulié (1632-1706) [C3 M2 Q T]
    Méditations de Saint Thomas (Toulouse, 1678)
    Divus Thomas sui interpres (Rome, 1692, 1709)

Thomas Ondermarck (d. 1709) [Q]
    Theses theologicae (Bruges, 1709)

Joseph Mayol (d. 1709) [Q]
    Summa moralis doctrinae thomisticae
        (Avignon, 1704)

John-Baptist Maderan (d. 1709) [Q]
    Supplementum clypei theologiae thomisticae

Alexander Pliny (1639-1709) [G3 Q]
    Quaestiones inter Thomistas et Molinistas
        (Lyons, 1666)
    Summae angelicae compendium (Lyons, 1680-81)
    Cursus philosophicus thomisticus
        (Cologne, 1693)

Germany and Austria

John Andrew Coppenstein (d. 1627) [Q]
  D. Thomae sermones (Mainz, 1616)
  Conciones ex D. Thomae commentariis
    (Mainz, 1616)

Sigismund Ferrarius (1589-1646) [M2 Q]
  Comm. ST
  Correctorium poematis super Summam

John Philip Fridt (d. 1654) [Q]
  Comm. ST

Leopold Luna (fl. 1658) [V2]
  Comm. I-II

Antonine Lehner (fl. 1658) [V2]
  Comm. I-II

Dominic Awrnhammer (d. 1660) [Q]
  Connubium pietatis cum sapientia (Douai, 1660)

Albert Zennerus (d. 1670) [Q]
  Armamentarium evangelico-thomisticum
    (Augsburg, 1665)

Henry Hilden (1642-82) [M2 Q]
  De physica praedeterminatione (Cologne, 1667)
  Comm. ST

Nicolaus Von Banckh (fl. 1687) [Q]
  Solemniores assertiones ex Summa D. Thomae
    (Salzburg, 1687)

Raymond Ortz (d. 1701) [Q]
  Cursus philosophicus (Vienna, 1673)
  Phoenix rediviva (Cologne, 1689)

Henry Van Hedickhuysen (1654-1701) [Q]
  Legalia angelica (Antwerp, 1689)
  De poenitentia (Antwerp, 1691)
  De sacramentis (Antwerp, 1693)

Theodolphus Cosyn (1659-1705) [Q]
    De jure et justitia (Louvain, 1690)
    Septem novae legis sacramenta (Louvain, 1697)
    De beatitudine et actibus humanis
        (Louvain, 1698)

Martin Wigandt (d. 1706) [Q]
    Tribunal confessariorum et ordinandorum
        (Augsburg, 1703)
    Tripartita universae philosophiae (Augsburg)

Albert Oswaldt (d. 1711) [Q]
    Spicilegium philosophicum (Cologne, 1697)
    Schola thomistica

Reginald Jung (d. 1711) [Q]
    Tractatlein von vier kleinen opusculis (1684)

                    Great Britain and Ireland

Didacus Arturus (fl. 1644) [M2 Q]
    Comm. ST

John Hecquet (fl. 1675) [Q]
    Comm. I-II (Rome, 1659)
    Synopsis physica (Rome, 1659)
    De fide, spe, et caritate (Rome, 1675)

John Baptist Hacket (d. 1676) [M2 Q]
    Comm. I-II (Rome, 1654)

Dominic Lynze (d. 1697) [Q]
    Summa philosophiae speculativae
        (Paris, 1666-86)

James Dillon (d. 1701) [Q]
    In epistolam sancti Paui ad Romanos
        (Louvain, 1701)

Gelasius MacMahon (d. 1703) [Q]
    Conclusiones theologicae (Louvain, 1683)

Gilbert Parker (1667-1707) [Q]
    Comm. I-II (Louvain, 1701)

John Roche (d. 1708) [Q]
   De poenitentia (Louvain, 1693)
   De actibus humanis (Louvain, 1694)
   De jure et justitia (Louvain)

Holland

Henry Hecktermans (1606-79) [Q]
   Compendium doctrinae Johannis a S. Thoma
     (Brussels, 1658)

Italy

John Dominic Montagnolus (fl. 1610) [Q]
   Defensiones philosophiae thomisticae
     (Venice, 1609)
   Defensiones theologicae D. Thomae
     (Naples, 1610)
   Philosophia naturalis (Naples, 1612)

Lactantius of Cremona (fl. 1610) [Q]
   Deipare Virginis encomium (Cremona, 1611)

John Saulius (d. 1611) [M2 Q]
   De libertate adversus Calvinum
   Comm. III

Raphael Ripa (1569-1611) [M2 Q]
   Commentaria Cajetani ad De ente (Rome, 1598)
   Cajetani ad primam partem (Venice, 1609)
   Comm. III

Girolamo Musitano (fl. 1612) [R9]
   De auxiliis (Messina, 1621)
   Theologicae disputationes (Messina, 1621)

Jerome Capredonius (fl. 1612) [M2 Q]
   De anima et De substantiis separatis
   Comm. I, III

Seraphinus Razzi (1531-1613) [Q]
   Conciones de peccato (1573)
   De substantia et cognitione angelorum (1585)
   La corona angelica

Thomas del Monacho (fl. 1613) [Q]
    Commentaria in Aristotelis philosophiam
    Comm. ST

Seraphinus Capponi (1536-1614) [C M2 Q T]
    Elucidationes formales in Summam (Venice, 1588)
    Theologia S. Thomae in compendium redacta
        (Venice, 1597)
    Indices S. Thomae (Padua, 1698)

Gaspar Carcano (d. 1615) [Q]
    Compendium Summae S. Thomae

Peter Martyr Festa (d. 1619?) [M Q]
    Comm. III

James of Rovigo (fl. 1620) [M2 Q]
    Comm. I, III

Jerome de Medices (d. 1622) [M2 Q R4]
    Formalis explicatio ST
        (Venice 1614-1617 and Salo 1622)

John Mary de Garexio (fl. 1622) [M2 Q]
    Comm. I, III

Peter Martyr Locatellus (d. 1625?) [M2 Q]
    Comm. I, III

Francis Jerome (fl. 1626) [Q]
    Commentaria Raphaelis Ripa in De ente
        (Rome, 1598)

Basil Spinula (d. 1627) [M2 Q]
    Controversiae in maximam partem Summae
    Questiones metaphysicae

Seraphinus Pascha (d. 1627) [M2 Q]
    Comm. III

Seraphinus Siccus (1560-1628) [Q]
    In De anima
    De SS. Trinitate ad mentem S. Thomae

Benedict Justiniani (fl. 1628) [M2 Q]
    Comm. III

Marcellus Levaretti (fl. 1628) [Q]
    Comm. III (Bologna, 1628)

Anthony Cellius (fl. 1629) [Q]
    De gratia ex S. Thomae theologia (Rome, 1629)

Vincent Giancardo (1570-1631) [M2 Q]
    Comm. I-II, II-II

John Ravotti (fl. 1631) [Q]
    Centones de D. Thomae translatione
        (Venice, 1631)

Francis Ghetius (d. 1639) [Q]
    Summa theologiae moralis (Piacenza, 1628-29)
    Thesaurus animae (Milan, 1639)

Latinus Paganus Ursinius (1610-41) [Q]
    Panegyris S. Thomae (Rome, 1633)

Matthew Anna (d. 1641) [Q]
    Il Tommaso d´Aquino trionfante: Tragedia
        (Palermo, 1641)

Michael Zanardi (1570-1642) [M2 Q]
    Comm. in libros Metaphysicae (Venice, 1615)
    Comm. I (Venice, 1620)
    Comm. III

Gregory Donatus (1579-1642) [Q]
    Orationes in laudem D. Thomae
    S. Thomae Summa theologica (Rome, 1618)

Bernardine Gauslinus (d. 1643) [Q]
    De laudibus Divi Thomae (Padua, 1604)

Dominic Gravina (d. 1643) [Q T]
    Summae compendium rhythmicum (Naples, 1625)
    Catholicae praescriptiones adversus haereticos
        (Naples, 1619-39)
    Cherubim Paradisi S. Thomas (Naples, 1641)

Hyacinth Jordanus a Sancta Agatha (fl. 1643) [Q]
    Theorica medicinae S. Thomae (Naples, 1634)

Bartholomew Marchi (d. 1644) [C]

John Paul Nazarius (1556-1645) [M2 Q W4]
    Comm. I (Venice, 1613)
    Comm. III (Venice and Cologne, 1620)
    De scriptis D. Thomae (Bologna, 1631)

Paul Minerva (d. 1645) [Q]
   In libros Aristotelis de philosophia naturali
      (Naples, 1615)

Remigius Scroffa (1583-1645) [Q]
   Quaestiones morales (Venice, 1640)

Gregory Cippullus (fl. 1647) [M2 Q]
   Comm. III (Rome, 1646)

Paul Zocca (d. 1648) [M2 Q]
   Controversia in primam et tertiam Summae partes

Thomas Turcus (1600-49) [M2 Q]
   Comm. I-II

John Baptist of Martinengo (d. 1649) [C]

John Baptist Silvester (fl. 1649) [Q]
   De sapientia S. Thomae (Perugia, 1645)

Maurice de Gregorio (d. 1651) [Q]
   Defensio D. Thomae
   Comm. SCG (Naples, 1644)
   Comm. Sent. (Naples, 1645)

Sanctes Franco (fl. 1653) [Q]
   Virginis Mariae rosarium (Naples, 1642)
   Symbolum apostolorum (Naples, 1647)
   Speculum quadragesimale (Naples, 1653)

Thomas Tomassonus (1615-54) [Q]
   Haeresis debellata (Rome, 1650)

John Thomas Gastaldi (d. 1655) [M2 Q]
   Symbolum apostolicum (Rome, 1629)
   De potestate angelica (Rome, 1650)
   Comm. I (Rome, 1651)

Hyacinth de Rugeriis (fl. 1655) [Q]
   Theologiae D. Thomae Summula (Rome, 1652)
   Defensorium D. Thomae (Naples, 1655)

Michael Borzinus (1602-56) [M2 Q]
   Comm. I, III

Joseph Mary Avila (1603?-56) [Q]
   Laudatio D. Thomae (Rome, 1634)

Francis Cavarricinus (d. 1656) [M2 Q]
    Comm. I

Thomas de Franciscis (d. 1656) [M2 Q]
    Comm. I, I-II, II-II

Louis Mary Calchi (fl. 1657) [M2 Q]
    Comm. ST
    Commentum super De ente

Xantes Mariales (1580?-1660) [M2 Q]
    Controversiae ad Summam S. Thomae
        (Venice, 1624)
    Quaestiones disputatae D. Thomae
        (Bologna, 1658)
    Biblioteca interpretum ad Summam (Venice, 1660)

Dominic Lionius (fl. 1660) [Q]
    Thomistica mathesis (Florence, 1660)

Mark Pius Pini (d. 1661) [Q]
    Sermon en la fiesta di S. Thomas

Jerome Fonseca (d. 1662) [M2 Q]
    Comm. I (published)

Giacomo Bruni (fl. 1665) [R9]
    Summulae (Messina, 1663)
    Summa philophica (Messina, 1663-67)

Ignatius Ciantes (1594-1667) [Q]
    Laudatio S. Thomae (Rome, 1615)

Dominic de Marinis (1599-1669) [M2 Q]
    Comm. ST (Lyons, 1663-68)

John Mary Bertinus (fl. 1669) [Q]
    Teologia mistica (Palermo, 1668)

Denys Leone of Lecce (d. 1670) [M2 Q]
    Opuscula logicalia (Lecce, 1665)
    Physicalia juxta mentem D. Thomae (Lecce, 1670)
    Comm. I (Lecce 1651-55 and Naples 1671)

Joseph Mary Ciantès (d. 1670) [Q T]
    Summa contra gentes hebraice (Rome, 1657)

Ambrose Lesaro de Belliquadro (fl. 1670) [Q]
    Tractactus de Sacramentis (Ticini Legii, 1670)

Hyacinth Balada de Morlupo (fl. 1670) [Q]
    Orationes in laudem D. Thomae

Reginald Lucarinus (d. 1671) [Q T]
    S. Thomae laudatio (Rome, 1622)
    Manuale controversiarum thomisticarum
        (Rome, 1666)

John Thomas Pozzobonelli (fl. 1671) [C M2 Q]
    Comm. I, III
    Super Aristotelis philosophiam

Agapito Ugone of Brescia (fl. 1672) [C]
    Super Aristotelis logicam

Felix Accorsi (fl. 1666-73) [C]

John Baptist Petrobelli (d. 1674) [M2 Q]
    Comm. III

Mark Ferro (1585-1675) [Q]
    In Aquinatem et Cajetanum elucidationes
        (Venice, 1656)

Vincent-Mary Fontana (d. 1675) [Q T]
    Epicinia sacra D. Thomae (Rome, 1670)

Vincent Persio (d. 1676) [Q]
    Sedes judicialis Salomonis (Naples, 1673)
    Samson salvatoris typus (Naples, 1676)

Peter Mary Passerinus de Sextula (1595-1677)
[M2 Q]
    Comm. II-II (Rome, 1663-65)
    Comm. III (Rome, 1669)

Joseph de Vita (d. 1677) [Q]
    De principio unde provenit peccatum
        (Palermo, 1665)
    De objecto logicae (Rome, 1670)

Augustine Cermelli (d. 1677) [C]
    Vita Thomae Aquinatis (Ferrara, 1648)

Leonard of Bassano (fl. 1677) [Q]
    D. Thomas laudatus (Rome, 1677)

Gabriel Marletta (fl. 1678) [M2 Q]
    Controversiae ad primam partem
        (Naples, 1662-67)
    Comm. I-II, II-II

Anthony Francis Fracassi (d. 1681) [M2 Q]
    Comm. III
    Oratio de laudibus S. Thomae
    La gran scienza di Tommaso (Rome, 1680)
    Panegyris epigrammatica in vitam D. Thomae
        (Rome, 1681)

Michael Archangel Rivetta (d. 1681) [Q]
    Comm. ST

Thomas Elias Ardizzonus (d. 1682) [M2 Q]
    Comm. ST

Hyacinth Libelli (d. 1684) [Q]
    De concursu Dei ad operationes liberas

Thomas Menghini (fl. 1684) [C]

Thomas Mary Giovi (fl. 1685) [Q]
    Physica Cajetani
    Metaphysica Cajetani

Dominic Thomas Manlelli (fl. 1686) [Q]
    De sacramento et virtute poenitentiae
        (Bologna, 1686)

Michael Pius Torrez (fl. 1687) [M2 Q]
    Comm. I (Bologna, 1672)

Vincent Jovaneti (fl. 1687) [M2 Q]
    Comm. ST (Asculi in Piceno)

Dominic Mary Pozzobonello (1603?-88) [M2 Q]
    Comm. I

Hyacinth Mazzucchi (fl. 1688) [C]

Innocent Pencini (1639-89?) [Q]
    Nova veteris legis galaxia (Venice, 1670)
    Nova evangelicae legis galaxia
        (Venice, 1678-85)

Angelus Julianus (fl. 1689) [Q]
    Apologeticum pro doctrina S. Thomae

Lawrence Mary Pisani (1650-90) [M2 Q]
   Gedeonis gladius: propositiones ab
      Innocentio XI damnatae angelici doctoris
      (Palermo, 1683)
   Comm. III

Raymond Capisucchi (1616-91) [Q]
   Controversiae theologicae (Rome, 1670)
   Appendices ad controverias theologicas
      (Rome, 1671)

Boniface Mary Grandi (1624-92) [M2 Q]
   Cursus Theologicus (Ferrara, 1692)

Julius Vincent Gentilis (d. 1694) [M2 Q]
   Comm. III

Seraphinus Piccinardi (1634-95) [M2 Q]
   Philosophia peripatetica christiana
      (Padua, 1671)
   De approbatione doctrinae S. Thomae
      (Padua, 1683)

Peter Martyr Bertagna (d. 1697) [Q]
   Cursus theologicus (Venice, 1697)

Dominic Ippolito Folegati (fl. 1699) [C]

Vincent Mary Sassetti (fl. 1700) [Q]
   La creazione mondiale (Palermo, 1692)

Joseph Mary Paltiniero (d. 1702) [Q W4]
   Vinea Moliniae demolita (Venice, 1683)
   Ars logica (Ferrara, 1694)
   Dissertationum trias (Padua, 1698)

Joseph-Mary Zucchi (d. 1703) [Q]
   La militia angelica (Naples, 1681)
   Metaphysica (Bologna, 1684)
   Dottrina cristiana (Rome, 1695)

Philip-Mary Grossi (d. 1704) [Q]
   Tractatus in theologiam moralem (Modena, 1694)
   Theologiae ethico-thomisticae epitome, I
      (Venice, 1700)

Peter-Martyr Petrucci (1644-1704) [Q]
   Lucerna moralis Aquinatici solis (Rome, 1698)

Joseph of Lucca (d. 1705) [Q]
    La Sapienza

Thomas-Mary Bosio (1627-1705) [Q]
    Tractatus in Summam S. Thomae

Daniel Danieli (d. 1706) [Q]
    Gemmae theologicae Aquinatis (Trent, 1694)

Julius-Mary Bianchi (1627-1707) [Q]
    Sacrae theologiae theses (Venice, 1656)

Thomas Borelli (d. 1708) [Q]
    Rosario meditato e recitato (Genoa, 1708)

Gabriel Valentino (1628?-1708) [Q]
    Opusculum de scientia Dei (Naples, 1700)

Hyacinth-Rose Cameroni (d. 1710) [Q]
    Philosophia aristotelica
    Fides catholica

Thomas Anthony Assanti (d. 1711) [Q]
    Comm. I

Dominic da Turro [C]

John Mary Borzinus [Q]
    Super S. Thomae De fato

                    New World

Ferdinand Bacan (fl. 1618) [M2 Q]
    Comm. I-II, III (Mexico)

John de Lorenzana (d. 1620?) [M2 Q]
    Comm. ST

Anthony de Peñaranda (fl. 1632) [Q]
    Panegirico de san Tomás

Cristóbal de Torres (d. 1653) [C6 Q]
    In laudem S. Thomae

Adrian de Alessio (fl. 1653) [Q]
    Vida de sancto Thomas (Madrid)

Francis a Cruce (d. 1654) [Q]
    In quaestiones disputatas S. Thomae
    Propositio theologica (Barcelona, 1636)

Anthony de Luque (d. 1655?) [Q]
    Arcana nova theologiae thomisticae

Balthasar Ortiz de Carrabeo (d. 1701) [Q]
    Medulla Angelici Doctoris

Francis Varo [L2]
    Prove della Religione

Raymond (del Valle?) [L2]
    La natura del corpo et dell'anima (1673)

                        Poland

Blase Pegaz (fl. 1610) [L]
    Quicquid scripsit D. Thomas verum est
    Theses concordiae libri arbitrii cum motione
        Dei (Poznan, 1610)

Severin Lubomlius (d. 1618) [C2 Q]
    Theatrum in scientia speculativa S. Thomae
        (Venice, 1597)
    Tabula Summae S. Thomae

Abraham Bzovius (1565?-1637) [Q]
    Comm. I, III
    S. Thomae Summa cum commentariis Cajetani

Raymond Madrowicz (fl. 1639) [L Q]
    Cicada rhythmica I (Lwow, 1639)

Fabian Bircovius (1566-1645) [Q]
    Orationes ecclestiasticae De S. Thoma
        (Cracow, 1622)

Nicholas of Mosciska (1587?-1645?) [C2 Q]
    Summa D. Thomae forma syllogistica
    Theologia moralis (Cracow, 1683)

Francis Albert Gabriecki (d. 1653) [Q]
    Compendium supplementi Summae (Paris, 1653)

Samuel Wierzchonski of Lublin (d. 1658) [C2 L Q]
    In libros Physicorum (Cologne, 1627)
    In De anima (Cologne, 1627)

Blase Krauzowski (fl. 1671) [L]
    Questio philosophica (Cracow, 1663)
    Doctor angelicus (Cracow, 1671)

Simon Stanislaus Makowski (fl. 1680) [L S2]
    Cursus philosophicus (1679-81)

S. T. Szulz-Pratnicki (fl. 1695) [L]
    Theses thomistico-philosophicae (Wroclaw, 1688)
    Compendium ST (Gdansk, 1694-95)

Thomas Szulc (d. 1705) [Q]
    Summa D. Thomae in compendium contracta
    Cursus theologicus (Danzig, 1696)

John-Alan Bardzinski (1657-1708) [C2 L Q]
    Breve compendium Summae Angelicae
        (Warsaw, 1705)

Ferdinand Ohm-Januszewski (1639-1712) [C2 L Q]
    Theologia moralis (Cracow, 1683)
    Sententiae morales (Cracow, 1687)
    Summa philosophica (Cracow, 1692)
    Comm. I

                    Portugal

Louis de Sottomaior (1526-1610) [F3]

Peter Martyr Lusitanus (d. 1615) [M2 Q]
    Comm. III

Vincent Pons (fl. 1615) [F3 M2 Q]
    Quaestiones philosophicae
        (Aix-en-Provence, 1615)
    Comm. III

Joseph de Sancta Maria (fl. 1625) [F3 Q]
    Tractatus thomisticus de libero arbitrio
        (Lisbon, 1625)

Ignatius Galvão (d. 1642) [Q]
    In commendationem D. Thomae
        (Evora 1625 and Lisbon 1635)

John of Portugal (1554-1644) [F3]

Francis d'Araujo (1580-1664) [F3 M2 Q]
    Comm. ST (Salamanca and Madrid, 1634-47)

Peter Magalhaens (1594-1675) [F3 M2 Q]
    Comm. I (Lisbon, 1666-70)

Dominic of St. Thomas (d. 1675) [F3 M2 Q]
    Comm. ST (Lisbon, 1670)

Francis Mexias [F3]

                        Sardinia

Francis Manca de Prado (fl. 1636) [Q]
    Aristotelis philosophiae expositio thomistica
        (Messina, 1636)

                        Spain

Francis of Avila (fl. 1604) [M2]
    Comm. I-II (Rome, 1599)

Anthony de Padilla (1554-1611) [M2]
    Comm. II-II

Raphael de la Torre (d. 1612) [M2 Q]
    Comm. II-II (Salamanca, 1611-12)

Diego Nuño Cabezudo (d. 1614) [M2 Q]
    Comm. III (Valladolid, 1601-09)
    Tractatio in tertiam partem Summae (Rome, 1682)

Francis de Zuñiga (d. 1614) [M2]
    Comm. I (Lyons, 1623)

Peter of Ledesma (d. 1616) [M2 Q]
    De matrimonii sacramento (Salamanca, 1592)
    Comm. I (Salamanca, 1596)
    Doctrina christiana (Salamanca, 1598)

Vincent Bernedo (d. 1619) [M2 Q]
    Comm. I, II-II

Anthony de Remesal (fl. 1619) [Q]
    Annotationes in sermones S. Thomae

John Gonzales de Albelda (d. 1622) [M2 Q]
    Comm. I (Complutum, 1621)

Michael Vasquez de Palilla (1559-1624) [M2]
    Comm. I, III

Blase Verdu a Sans (d. 1625?) [M2 Q]
    Disputatio de rebus universalibus
        (Valencia, 1593)
    Comm. I (Tarragona, 1602)
    Commentaria in logicam Aristotelis
        (Barcelona, 1614)

Balthazar Navarrette (fl. 1625) [M2 Q]
    Controversiae in Divi Thomae defensionem
        (Valladolid, 1605-34)

Vincent Gomez (1560?-1626) [Q]
    Relacion de las famosas fiestas
        (Valencia, 1602)
    Govierno de principes (Valencia, 1626)

Lawrence Gutierrez (d. 1627) [Q]
    Comm. I

Thomas Malvenda (fl. 1628) [M2 Q]
    Comm. III

Thomas de Lemos (d. 1629) [M2 Q]
    Comm. I-II (Louvain, 1702)

Peter of Herrera (1548-1630) [M2 Q]
    In De Trinitate D. Thomae (Pavia, 1627)

Thomas de Torres (d. 1630) [M2 Q]
    Comm. III

Diego Alvarez (d. 1635) [M2 Q]
    Comm. I-II (Trani, 1617)
    De incarnatione (Lyons, 1614)

Andrew de Luna (fl. 1635) [Q]
    Comm. I-II (Antwerp, 1670)

Cosmas Morelles (d. 1636) [M2 Q W4]
    D. Thomae operum editio nova (Antwerp, 1612)
    Comm. III

John Gonzales of Leon (fl. 1636) [M2]
    Comm. I-II (Liège, 1708)

Gregory Martinez (1575-1637) [M2 Q]
    Comm. I-II
        (Valladolid 1617, Toledo 1622, Valladolid
        1637)

J. A. Uson (1594?-1638) [M2]
    Comm. I

Nicholas Riccardi (1585-1639) [Q]
    Disputationes in D. Thomam

John Biescas (d. 1640) [M2 Q]
    Apologia pro doctrina S. Thomae
    Comm. I-II

John de Claveria (fl. 1640) [Q]
    Santo Tomas y su doctrina (Saragossa, 1638)

Didacus Ortiz (fl. 1640) [Q]
    Quaestiones in logicam (Seville, 1640)
    Cursus philosophicus Angelico-thomisticus
        (Kempten, Bavaria, 1667)

Cosmas of Lerma (d. 1642) [M2 Q]
    Comm. III
    Compendium summularum Dominici de Soto
        (Burgos, 1641)

John (Poinsot) of St. Thomas (1589-1644) [M2 Q T]
    Comm. ST (Complutum 1637, Lyons 1643, Madrid
       1645-56, Paris 1667)
    Speculum sine macula (Cologne, 1658)
    Cursus philosophicus (Paris, 1883)

Mark Serra (1581-1645) [M2 Q]
    Comm. ST (Valencia, 1653)

Thomas Villar (d. 1647) [M2 Q]
    Summae controversiarum in Summam
       (Barcelona, 1638-47)

John Alphonse Baptista (fl. 1648) [M2 Q]
    Comm. I-II (Lyons, 1648)

Anthony Perez (1599-1649) [C6 M2]
    Comm. I (Rome, 1656)
    Comm. II, III (Lyons, 1669)

Francis de Oviedo (1602-51) [M2]
    Comm. I (Lyons, 1646)
    Comm. II-II (Lyons, 1646)
    Tractatus theologiae (Lyons, 1651)

Sebastian de Oquendo (d. 1651) [M2 Q]
    Theologia scholastica
    Theologia moralis

Gaspar Ruiz (d. 1652) [M2 Q]
    Comm. III (Valladolid, 1652)

Jerome Vives (fl. 1654) [M2 Q]
    De primatu divinae libertatis (Valentia, 1654)

Peter de Tapia (1582-1657) [M2 Q]
    Comm. I, III
    Catena moralis doctrinae
       (Seville 1654-57, Madrid 1664)

Gundisalvus de Arriaga (d. 1657) [Q T]
    Santo Tomas de Aquino (Madrid, 1648)

Alphonse Miguel (fl. 1658) [M2 Q]
    Comm. I (Complutum, 1658)

Didacus Ramirez (d. 1660) [M2 Q]
    Joannis a Sancto Thoma Commentaria in Summam
       (Madrid, 1645)

Barnabas Gallego de Vera (d. 1661?) [Q]
    Controversiae in defensionem D. Thomae
        (Madrid, 1623)

Didacus de Morales (fl. 1662) [Q]
    In laudem D. Thomae (Naples, 1662)

Thomas de Vallgornera (1595?-1665) [Q]
    Mystica theologia D. Thomae (Barcelona, 1662)

Peter de Villamayor (fl. 1665) [Q]
    Articulorum fidei expositio (Madrid, 1665)

John Martinez de Prado (d. 1668) [M2 Q]
    Controversiae metaphysicales (Complutum, 1649)
    Comm. III (Complutum, 1654)

Maurice de Lezana (d. 1668) [M2 Q]
    Comm. I (Madrid, 1668)

Anthony Salcedo (fl. 1670) [M2 Q]
    Comm. I (Madrid)

Francis of Ayllón (fl. 1671) [Q]
    Clypeum Thomisticum

Peter de Godoy (d. 1677) Cardinal [M2 Q]
    Disputationes in Summam (Osma, 1666-72)

Vincent Ferrer (d. 1682) [M2 Q]
    Comm. I, I-II, II-II
        (Salamanca 1675-90, Rome 1669)

Hyacinth de Parra (1619-84) [Q]
    Censura in disputationes Petri de Godoy
        (Osma, 1672)

Francis de Relux (d. 1686) [M2 Q]
    Comm. ST

John de Ribas y Carrasquilla (1612-87) [Q]
    Defensa de la doctrina del Angelico doctor
        (Madrid, 1663)

Peter de Matilla (fl. 1696) [M2 Q]
    Comm. III

Francis Perez de la Serna (d. 1701) [Q]
    Resolutiones ethicae et christiano-politicae
    Tractatus de merito justi
    De voluntate Dei

Raymond Costa (1651-1703) [Q]
    Biblia D. Thomae (Barcelona, 1676)

Emmanuel Voloso (1630-1706) [Q]
    Comm. I

John-Baptist Escuder (d. 1706) [Q]
    Comm. ST

Vincent of Blanès (d. 1707) [Q]
    Vida del Angelico Doctor (Valencia, 1695)

Anthony Irribarren (1655-1710) [Q]
    Philosophici cursus

Alphonse Manrique (d. 1711) [Q]
    Tractatus de orationis conditionibus (Venice)

Francis Carrasco (d. 1712) [Q]
    Dubia in sacra theologia (Valladolid, 1689)
    Comm. ST

Adrian Perez de Alecio [T]
    El Angelico (Madrid, 1645)

                    AUGUSTINIANS

Giles de Praesentatione et Fonseca (fl. 1600) [M2]
    Comm. I-II (Coimbra, 1609-15)

John Du Puy (fl. 1600) [M2]
    Comm. I

Gregory Falconi (fl. 1612) [M2]
    Reconciliatio inter D. Thomam et Aegidium
        Columnium (Rimini, 1612)

Michael Salon (d. 1620) [M2]
    Comm. II-II (Valencia, 1581)

John Puteanus (d. 1623) [M2]
   Comm. ST (Toulouse, 1627)

Basil Pontius (1569-1629) [M2]
   Comm. ST (Salamanca, 1627 or 1628)

John Zapata et Sandoval (d. 1630) [M2]
   Comm. I

Martin of Albitz (d. 1633) [M2]
   Comm. I (Complutum, 1632)

Michael Paludanus (d. 1652) [M2]
   Comm. I-II (Louvain, 1664)

Thomas of Herrera (1585-1654) [M2]
   Comm. I

Legros (fl. 1672) [M2]
   Comm. I-II

Augustine Gibbon (d. 1676) [G3]
   Speculum theologicum

John De Vita (d. 1677) [M2]
   Comm. I (Palermo, 1665)

Nicholas Gigos (fl. 1677) [M2]
   Comm. III

Joseph of Cordoba [M2]
   Comm. ST

William Farinoni [M2]
   Disputatio inter D. Thomam et Aegidium Romanum

BENEDICTINES

John Alphonse Curiel (d. 1609) [G3 M2]
   Comm. I-II (Douai 1618, Antwerp 1621)

James Carolus (fl. 1630) [M2]
   Comm. I, II-II

Charles Jacobus (d. 1661) [M2]
   Comm. II-II
   Comm. III (Salzburg, 1642)

Maurus Oberascher (fl. 1664) [M2]
    Comm. II-II, III

Bernard Weibl (fl. 1664) [M2]
    Comm. I, I-II, III

Didacus Pacheco de Silva (d. 1677) [M2]
    Comm. I (Madrid, 1663-65)
    Comm. I-II (Madrid, 1669)

Alphonse Stadelmayer (1610-83) [M2]
    Comm. II-II (Salzburg, 1651)

Augustine Reding (1625-92) [M2]
    Comm. ST (Salzburg, 1787)

Honorius Aigner (1651-1701) [M2]
    Comm. I-II, II-II

Paul Mezger (1637-1702) [M2 W]
    Comm. ST (Augsburg, 1695)

Celestine Sfondratus [T]
    Innocentia vindicata (St. Gall, 1695)

CAPUCHINS

Louis of Caspe (d. 1641) [M2]
    Comm. I (Lyons, 1641)

John Mary Zamora (d. 1649) [M2]
    Comm. I (Venice, 1626)

CARMELITES

Paul a Conceptione (d. 1617) [G3]

Peter Cornejo de Pedrosa (d. 1618) [M2]
    Comm. ST (Bamberg, 1671)

Thomas de Jesus (d. 1627) [M2]
    Comm. II-II (Cologne, 1684)

Anthony de la Madre de Dios (1583-1637) [C7 C8]
    Cursus artium (1624-28)
    Cursus theologiae (1631, 1637)

Valentine Mandoli (1572-1640) [C]

Ferdinand a Jesu (d. 1644) [M2]
    Comm. I-II (Coimbra, 1606)
    Comm. III (Baeza, 1613)

Dominic of St. Teresa (1604-60) [C7]
    Cursus theologiae (1631-1712)

Michael a SS. Trinitate (1588-1661) [C8 H3]
    Cursus artium (1624-28)

Daniel a S. Josepho (d. 1666) [M2]
    Comm. ST (Caen, 1643)

Andrew Kochanowski (1618-67) [L]
    Metaphysica (Cracow, 1679)

Gabriel a S. Vincentio (d. 1671) [M2]
    Comm. ST (Rome, 1664-66)

Philip a SS. Trinitate (d. 1671) [M2]
    Comm. ST (Lyons, 1653)

Joseph of the Holy Spirit (1609-74) [F3]

Andrew of the Mother of God (d. 1674) [C7]
    Cursus theologiae moralis (1665-1724)

Andrew a Cruce (d. 1675) [M2]
    Comm. I, I-II (Genoa, 1650-56)

Francis of Jesus and Mary (d. 1677) [C7]
    Cursus theologiae moralis (1665-1724)

Raymond Lumbier (d. 1684) [M2]
    Comm. I (Saragossa, 1680)

Charles de Brias (d. 1686) [M2]
    Comm. I (Douai, 1670)

Blase a Conceptione (1603-1694) [C8 M2 W]
    Cursus artium (1624-28)
    Comm. I-II (Paris, 1647)
    Comm. Metaphysica (Lyons, 1651)

Anthony of St. John the Baptist (1641-99) [C7]
    Cursus theologiae (1641-1712)

John of the Annunciation (1633-1701) [C7 C8]
    Cursus artium (1624-28)
    Cursus theologiae (1679-94)

Benedict Zoccolati (fl. 1706) [C]
    Logica et metaphysica

Dominic of Jesus [M2]

John Feyxoo de Villalobos [C3]

CISTERCIANS

Peter of Lorca (d. 1606) [M2]
    Comm. I-II (Complutum, 1609)
    Comm. II-II (Madrid; 1614)
    Comm. III (Complutum, 1616)

Francis Cabreiro (fl. 1609) [M2]
    Comm. I

Marsilius Vasquez (d. 1611) [M2]
    Comm. I-II

Angelus Manrique (1577?-1649) [M2]
    Comm. I

Chrysostom Cabero (d. 1650) [M2]
    Comm. I-II

Peter de Orviedo (d. 1651) [M2]
    Comm. I, I-II

Caramuel Lobkovitz (1606-82) [M2]
    Comm. ST

HIERONYMITES

John of Toledo (d. 1672) [M2]
    Comm. I (Leon, 1672)

Peter de Cabrera [M2]
    Comm. III (Cordoba, 1602)

                    JESUITS

                    Belgium

P. Roest (fl. 1610) [M2]
    Comm. I, III

John Deckers (d. 1619) [M2]
    Comm. ST (Douai, 1589-94)

Leonard Lessius (1554-1623) [M2]
    Comm. II-II (Louvain, 1605)
    Comm. I-II (Venice, 1617)
    Comm. III (Louvain, 1645)

Giles de Coninck (1571-1633) [M2]
    Comm. III (Antwerp, 1645)

Thomas Bacon (1592-1637) [M2]
    Comm. I, III

Christopher Mauritius (fl. 1656) [M2]
    Comm. III

Paul Rosmer (d. 1664) [M2]
    Comm. III (Graz, 1661)

Thomas van Nevelle (1618-72) [M2]
    Comm. I, III

Stephen Tucci [P9]
    De legibus

                    Bohemia

John Molitor (fl. 1652) [M2]
    Comm. III

Rodr. de Arriaga (d. 1667) [M2]
    Comm. ST (Lyons, 1643-55)

Charles de Grobbendonck (1600-72) [M2]
    Comm. I, II-II

China

Gabriel de Magalhaens (1609-77) [L2]
    Translated ST (Peking, 1654-78)

Louis Buglio (1606-82) [F3 M2]
    Chinese translation of ST (Peking, 1654-78)

France

Philip Monce (d. 1619) [M2]
    Comm. I (Paris, 1622)

John Prevost (d. 1634) [M2]
    Comm. III (Douai, 1629)
    Comm. I (Douai, 1631)
    Comm. I-II (Douai, 1637)

G. de la Porte (1556-1635) [M2]
    Comm. I

Andrew Duval (d. 1637) [G3 M2]
    Comm. ST

Claude Tiphaine (1571-1641) [M2]
    Comm. I (Reims, 1640)

Nicholas Ysambert (1569-1642) [G3]
    Comm. ST (Paris, 1639)

Jo. Phelippeau (1577-1645) [M2]
    Comm. on Osee (Paris, 1636)

Denis Petavius (1583-1652) [M2]
    Comm. I (Paris, 1643-50)

Bernard de Aldrete (d. 1657) [M2]
    Comm. III (Lyons, 1652)
    Comm. I (Lyons, 1662)

George Rhodes (1597-1661) [M2]
    Comm. ST (Lyons, 1661-64)

John Martinon (1586-1662) [M2]
    Comm. ST (Bordeaux, 1644)

L. Le Mairat (d. 1664) [M2]
    Disputationes in ST (Paris, 1633)

Francis Annat (1590-1670) [M2]
    Comm. I (Toulouse, 1645)
    Comm. I-II (Paris, 1666)

                Germany, Austria, Switzerland

John Busaeus (d. 1611) [M2]
    Comm. I-II (Mainz, 1577)

Sebastian Heissius (d. 1614) [H3 M2]
    Theses
    De sacrificio missae (Munich, 1605)

John Moquettius (fl. 1617) [M2]
    Comm. I, II-II

George Kern (1572-1619?) [M2]
    Comm. II-II

G. Eberhard (1555-1621) [M2]
    Comm. I, I-II

Martin Becanus (d. 1624) [M2]
    Comm. I (Wurzburg 1599 and Mainz 1611)

James Bidermann (fl. 1624) [M2]
    Comm. II-II, III

Maximilian Buscher (fl. 1629) [M2]
    Comm. I, I-II

Adam Tanner (1571-1632) [M2]
    Comm. ST (Ingoldstadt, 1618)
    Supplementum (Ingoldstadt, 1620)

John Theodore Lennep (d. 1639) [M2]
    Comm. I-II, III

Adam Burghaber (fl. 1649) [M2]
    Comm. I

Wolfgang Gravenegg (1590-1650) [M2]
   Comm. I (Dillingen, 1624)
   Commentarius in S. Thomam (Dillingen, 1625)
   Comm. I-II (Munich, 1627-28)

George Stengel (1585-1651) [M2]
   Comm. I, III

Maximilian Reichenberger (fl. 1652) [M2]
   Comm. III

Simon Felix (1583-1656) [M2]
   Comm. I

Max van der Sandt (d. 1656) [M2]
   Comm. I (Mainz, 1624)
   Comm. III

Conrad Horsaun (fl. 1661) [M2]
   Comm. III

Zacharias Ignatius Trinkellius (1602-65) [M2]
   Comm. I (Graz, 1636)

Paul Grandinger (1602-70) [M2]
   Comm. II-II

Isaias Molitor (1607-78) [M2]
   Comm. I

Lawrence Gerwig (1626-81) [M2]
   Comm. I-II (Freiburg i. B., 1666)
   Comm. II-II (Dillingen, 1669)
   Comm. III (Dillingen, 1670)

James Prugger (fl. 1681) [M2]
   Comm. I-II

James Illsung (1632-95) [M2]
   Comm. I, I-II, II-II

Ferdinand Krimer (1639-1703) [M2]
   Comm. II-II (Graz, 1691)
   Comm. III (Graz, 1691)

George Prugger [M2]
   Comm. I

Great Britain

William Creitton (d. 1615) [M2]
    Comm. I

Thomas Compton-Carleton (1591?-1666) [M2]
    Comm. ST (Liege, 1658-62)

Joseph Simonis (1595-1671) [M2]
    Comm. I
    Comm. II-II

Ireland

Stephen White (fl. 1614) [M2]
    Comm. III

Italy

Basil Alamannus (fl. 1612) [M2]
    Comm. I, I-II, III

Jerome Bellius (fl. 1612) [M2]
    Comm. III

Francis Albertini (1552-1619) [M2 R9]
    Comm. I (Naples, 1606)
    Comm. III (Lyons, 1616)

Saint Robert Bellarmine (1542-1621) Cardinal [M2]
    Comm. I, I-II, II-II

Joseph Ragusa (d. 1624) [M2]
    Comm. III (Lyons, 1619-20)

Peter Algona (d. 1624) [M2]
    Compendium ST (Rome, 1619)

Cosmo Alemanni (1559-1634) [N2 S6]
    Summa philosophiae (Pavia, 1618-23)

Stephen Bubalus de Cancellariis (d. 1634) [M2]
    Comm. I (Lyons, 1622)

Francis Paone (1569-1637) [R9]
   Summa ethicae (Naples, 1617)
   Introductio in sacram doctrinam (Naples, 1623)

Jerome Fasolus (d. 1639) [M2]
   Comm. I (Lyons, 1623-36)

Joseph Agostini (1573-1643) [M2]
   Comm. I (Palermo, 1639-43)

Anthony Mangilio (1576-1644) [M2]
   Comm. I, II-II, III

Terence Alciati (1570-1651) [M2]
   Comm. I, I-II, II-II

Gavinus Carta (d. 1653) [H3 M2]
   Comm. I

Sfortia Pallavicino (d. 1667) [M2]
   Comm. I-II (Lyons, 1653)

John Baptist Giattini (1601-72) [M2]
   Comm. I-II

Silvester Maurus (1619-87) [M2]
   Comm. ST (Rome, 1687)

Joseph Mary de Requesens (1612-90) [M2]
   Comm. I-II (Palermo 1659 and Rome 1675)

Achilles Gagliardi [P9]
   Comm. I-II, II-II

                        Mexico

John Ledesma (1575-1637) [M2]
   Comm. ST

                        Peru

John Perez de Menacho (1565-1626) [M2]
   Summa theologiae S. Thomae

Leonard Penafiel (1597-1657) [M2]
    Comm. I (Lyons, 1663-66)
    Comm. II-II (Lyons, 1668)
    Comm. III

Joseph of Aguilar (1652-1708) [M2]
    Comm. I (Cordoba, Argentina, 1731)

                          Poland

Michael Ortiz (1560-1638) [M2]
    Comm. I

Casimir Wolski-Ogonczk (d. 1690) [C2 M2]
    Comm. I (Poznan, 1695)

John Morawski (1631-1700) [C2 L M2]
    Philosophiae principia (Poznan, 1661)
    Comm. II-II, III (Kalisz, 1681)

                          Portugal

Nicholas Godigno (d. 1616) [M2]
    Comm. I

Francis Soares (1605-59) [M2]
    Comm. I

Bento Pereira (1605-81) [F3]

Augustine Laurenco (fl. 1690) [F3 M2]
    Comm. I (Leodii Eburonum, 1690)
    Comom. I-II (Leodii Eburonum, 1692)

                          Spain

Jo. de Salas (d. 1612) [M2]
    Comm. I-II (Barcelona 1607-09 and Lyons 1611)
    Comm. II-II (Lyons, 1617)

M. Gomez (fl. 1622) [M2]
    Comm. ST

Didacus Ruiz de Montoya (1562-1623) [M2]
    Comm. I (Lyons, 1625-31)

Jo. Mariana (1536-1624) [M2]
    Comm. I

Luke Guadin (fl. 1629) [M2]
    Comm. III

Thomas de Ituren (d. 1630) [M2]
    Comm. I (Madrid, 1619)

Michael de Espinosa (d. 1630) [M2]
    Comm. I

James Granado (1572-1632) [M2]
    Comm. ST (Seville and Granada, 1623-33)

George Hemelman (d. 1637) [M2]
    Comm. I (Granada, 1637)

Peter Hurtado de Mendoza (1578-1651) [M2]
    Comm. I, III

Francis of Lugo (d. 1652) Cardinal [M2]
    Comm. I (Lyons, 1647)

Louis Torres (d. 1655) [M2]
    Comm. II-II (Lyons, 1617)

P. of Aviles (fl. 1664) [M2]
    Comm. ST

Anthony Bernard Quiros (1613-68) [M2]
    Comm. I (Lyons, 1654)
    Comm. I-II, III

Caspar de Ribandeneira (d. 1675) [M2]
    Comm. I (Complutum, 1653)
    Comm. I-II (Comoplutum, 1655)

Augustine Herrera (1623-84) [M2]
    Comm. I (Complutum, 1671-75)

Philip of Aranda (1642-95) [M2]
    Comm. III (Saragossa, 1691)
    Comm. I (Saragossa, 1693)
    Comm. I-II (Saragossa, 1694)

James Alvarez de Paz [M2]
    Compendium ST

John Vincente [M2]
    Comm. I

MERCEDARIANS

Francis Zumel (d. 1607) [M2]
    Comm. I (Salamanca, 1585)
    Comm. I-II (Salamanca, 1594)

John Prudentius (d. 1660) [M2]
    Comm. III (Lyons, 1654)

ORATORIANS

Blessed Juvenal Ancina (d. 1604) [P9]
    Lectiones theologicae

Renoult (fl. 1635) [M2]
    Comm. III

Caesar Becilli (1580-1649) [P9]
    Compendium I
    Tabula ST

Odorico Rinaldi (d. 1681) [P9]
    Comm. I

Nicholas Lili [P9]
    Lectiones theologicae

SERVITES

Girolamo John Gambi (fl. 1614-37) [C]

Girolamo Scarpari (d. 1650) [C]
    Super doctrinam Henrici de Gandavo (1646)

Denis Borsetti (d. 1654) [C]

Hyppolytus Bazzani (d. 1660) [C]

Gerard Baldi (d. 1660) [G]
    Catholica monarchia Christi

OTHERS

Belgium

Otto Vaenius [T]
    Vita D. Thomae (Antwerp, 1610)

John van Malderon (1563-1633) [G3 M2]
    Comm. II-II (Antwerp, 1616)
    Comm. I-II (Antwerp, 1623)
    Comm. I (Antwerp, 1634)

John Wiggers (1571-1639) [G3 M2]
    Comm. ST (Louvain, 1631-41)

William Merchier (1572-1639) [M2]
    Comm. I, III

Francis Sylvius of Brania (1581-1649) [G3 M2]
    Comm. ST (Douai, 1620)

Anthony Ruteau (Minim) (d. 1657) [M2]
    Comm. I (1653)

Gerard de Vries [M2]
    Selected questions of ST

Bohemia

Matthew Werner (1610-84) [M2]
    Comm. II-II

China

Francis Sambiasi (fl. 1624) [L2]
    De anima (Kia-Ting, 1624)

Francis Futardo (fl. 1630) [L2]
    De coelo et mundo
    De praedicamentis

Leo Ly-Chih-Tsao (fl. 1630) [L2]
   De coelo et muhndo
   De praedicamentis

Alphonse Vagoni (fl. 1635) [L2]
   Ethica
   Politica
   Questioni filosofiche

                      England

Matthew Kellison (d. 1641) [M2]
   Comm. III (Douai, 1633)

John Norris (1656?-1711) [R5]
   Reason and Faith (1697)
   The Theory of the Ideal World (1701-04)
   The Immortality of the Soul (1705)

                      France

J. Hennequin (fl. 1612) [M2]
   Comm. III

William Estius (1542-1613) [G3 M2]
   Comm. ST (Douai, 1613)

Melchior Raphael (fl. 1614) [M2]
   Comm. I-II

Rambert (fl. 1614) [M2]
   Comm. ST

Magesc (fl. 1621) [M2]
   Comm. II-II

Philip of Gamaches (1568-1625) [G3 M2]
   Comm. ST (Paris, 1634)

Peter a S. Joseph (fl. 1633) [M2 T]
   Comm. I-II (Lyons, 1633)
   Defensio S. Thomae (Paris, 1643)

George Colvenerius (d. 1649) [M2]
   Comm. I-II, II-II

Louis Bail (1610-69) [M2 T]
   La théologie affective (Paris, 1654)

Louis Thomas (fl. 1676) [M2]
   Comm. I

James Benignus Bossuet (1627-1704) [S6]
   Traité de la connaissance
   Traité du libre arbitre

A. Armand [T]
   Vindiciae S. Thomae (1656)

Andrew Duvallius [M2]
   Comm. ST (Paris, 1636)

Matthias Rorer [M2]
   Comm. ST

N.C.M. de Hauteville [T]
   La théologie angélique (Lyons, 1657)

N. de la Lanne [T]
   Vindiciae S. Thomae (1656)

N. de Marandé [M2]
   Abridgement of ST (Paris, 1649)

P. Nicole [T]
   Vindiciae S. Thomae (1656)

P. Tiphane [T]
   De hypostasi et persona (Pont-à-Mousson, 1634)

                        Germany

Marianus Schwab (d. 1650?) [M2]
   Comm. I, I-II, III

Francis Sens (fl.1659) [M2]
   Comm. III

Rabanus Hirschbeindtner (fl. 1667) [M2]
    Comm. II-II

James Horus [M2]
    Comm. I-II

                          Italy

Alphonse de Marcho Aversano (fl. 1605) [M2]
    Edited Formalitates of Matthias Aquarius
        (Naples, 1605)

Sante Pasti (1523-1623) [C]

Alphonse Bavosi (Can. Reg. of the Holy Saviour)
(d. 1628) [M2]
    Comm. I
    Cosmo Alemanni (1559-1634)

Ambrose Machin de Aquena (fl. 1634) [M2]
    Comm. I (Cagliari, 1634)

Lanardi (d. 1642) [R4]

Efisio Joseph de Soto Regali (fl. 1664) [M2]
    Comm. II-II

Maurice a Gregorio (d. 1666) [M2]
    Comm. ST (Naples, 1645)

Charles Tomasi (Theatine) (d. 1675) [M2]
    Comm. ST (Rome, 1656)

Almerio Passarelli (d. 1682) [C]

Stephen Spinula (Clerk Regular of Somascha)
(d. 1682) [M2]
    Comm. I (Pavia, 1681)

John Andrew Negrisoli (fl. 1673-94) [C]

Jerome Casanate (1620-1700) Cardinal [C3]

A. Bartolini [T]
    S. Tommaso e Dante (1894)

Balthazar of St. Catherine of Siena [T]
   Splendori riflessi (Bologna, 1671)

Candido Giacomo of Syracuse [P9]
   Compendium ST

J. Maffeus [W]
   Sylva distinctionum thomisticarum (Pisa, 1677)

Louis Carbone [T]
   Catalogus interpretum Summae (Cologne, 1618)

P. Etiro [T]
   Vita di Tommaso (Venice, 1630)

P. Frigerio [T]
   Vita di S. Tommaso (Rome, 1615)

                         New World

John Montaña (fl. 1654) [C6]
   Comm. I-II

Mendoza y Espleta (fl. 1661) [C6]
   Comm. II-II

Charles de Siguenza y Gongora [G4]

John Martinez de Ripalda [C6]
   De usu et abusu doctrinae D. Thomae
      (Liège, 1704)

Sister Juana Inés de la Cruz [G4]
   Summulae

                         Poland

Sebastian Stryjewicz (fl. 1670) [M2]
   Comm. II-II

Dobrocieski [S2]

Nic. Cichovius [T]
   De immaculata conceptione (Poznan, 1651)

Nicholas Eichof [T]
   De immaculata conceptione (Poznan, 1651)

Theophilus Rutka [T]
   Ecclesia graeca (Lublin, 1694)

Vladislav a Conceptione [T]
   Enconium (Warsaw, 1682)

                    Portugal

Manuel da Natividad (1549-1629) Our Lady of Ransom
[F3]
   Philosophia

Francis of St. Augustine of Macedo (1596-1681)
[F3 M2]
   Comm. I-II (Padua, 1671-80)

Matthew Sousa [F3]

                    Russia

Nicholas Kursulas (d. 1652) [R7]
   Theologia (Zante, 1862)

                    Spain

Caspar Ram (fl. 1611) [M2]
   Comm. I-II (Huesca, 1611)

Francis Pena (1540?-1612) [M2]
   Comm. I-II

Andrew Henriquez de Villegas (fl. 1618) [M2]
   Comm. I (Complutum, 1618)

Louis de Montesinos (d. 1623) [G3 M2]
   Comm. I-II (Complutum, 1621)

Alva y Astorga [T]
   De operibus S. Thomae (Brussels, 1663)

Anthony de la Parra et Arteaga [M2]
   Comm. III (Madrid, 1667-68)

Salazar [M2]
   Comm. I-II (Barcelona, 1607)

Eighteenth Century

DOMINICANS

Belgium

Martin Harney (1634-1704) [Q]
    Oratio in laudem S. Thomae (Brussels, 1683)

Gregory de le Wincque (fl. 1710) [Q]
    Oratio de doctore angelico (Tournai, 1681)

Jerome Henneguier (1633-1712) [Q]
    Vanitas triumphorum (Douai, 1670)
    Oratio in laudem S. Thomae (Antwerp, 1702)

Norbert Delbecque (1651-1714) [Q]
    Vindiciae gratiae divinae (Brussels, 1711)
    Comm. ST
    Summa ad antiquiores codices recognita

Dominic Maloteau (d. 1715) [Q]
    Theologia (Douai, 1710)

Francis Janssens-Elinga (1635-1715) [Q]
    Authoritas Divi Thomae (Ghent, 1664)
    Theses theologice de scientia Dei (Antwerp)
    Theses theologicae de SS. Trinitate
        (Antwerp, 1680)

James Hyacinth Serry (fl. 1720) [M2 Q W]
    Schola thomistica vindicata (Cologne, 1706)

Gregory Van Hoorde (1679-1721) [Q T]
    Vita Sancti Thomae de Aquino (Ghent, 1718)

Francis D´Enghein (1648-1722) [Q T]
    De actibus humanis (Louvain, 1686)
    De sacramentis (Louvain, 1688)
    Theologia (Louvain, 1699)

William Poelman Ilander (fl. 1722) [Q]
    S. Thomas eiusque discipuli vindicati
        (Louvain, 1721)

Norbert Van Bilsen (fl. 1722) [Q]
    Epistola expostularia (Douai, 1684)

Francis Van Ranst (1672-1727) [Q]
    Compendium controversiarum (Antwerp, 1709)
    Veritas in medio (Antwerp, 1715)
    Lux fidei (Antwerp, 1717)

Hyacinth Van Huysen (1664-1729) [Q]
    Theologia miscellanea (Antwerp, 1711)

Hyacinith De Baets (d. 1731) [Q]
    Theses theologicae
        (Antwerp 1692-93, Louvain 1705-09)

Thomas Du Jardin (1653-1733) [Q]
    Theses theologicae (Louvain, 1691-97)

John Poelman (1677-1736) [Q]
    Theses theologicae (Liège, 1709)
    Theses theologicae (Roermond)
    Theses theologicae (Louvain)

Charles René Billuart (1685-1757) [M2 Q]
    De mente ecclesiae (Liège, 1715)
    Le thomisme vengé (Brussels, 1720)
    Comm. ST (Leodii, 1746-51)

                        Bohemia

Norbert Schneider (d. 1711) [K3 Q]
    Dies cinerum dies Aquinatis (Prague, 1692)

Albert Henigar (1640-1714) [Q]
    Paradisus voluptatis (Prague, 1671)

Anthony Pfrenger (1647-1717) [K3 Q]
    Dialectica major
    Cursus philosophicus

Reginald Lautterbach (1657-1720) [K3 Q]
    Comm. I

Francis Gottol (d. 1722) [K3 Q]

Martin Schindler (d. 1722) [K3 Q]

Thomas Brabant (1663-1727) [Q]
    Comm. I

Wenceslaus Ficklscher (1663-1727) [Q]
    Tractatus de legibus

Wenceslaus Oew (1670-1727) [K3 Q]
    Philosophia naturalis aristotelica
    Metaphysica Aristotelis
    Tractatus de sacramento poenitentiae
      (Brno, 1705)

Albino Proedl (1672-1727) [K3 Q]
    Institutiones dialecticae

Cyprian Liesch (1672-1729) [K3 Q]
    Comomentaria in libros Physicorum
    Tractatus de jure et justitia
    Commentaria in metaphysicam

Albert Panhans (1659-1731) [K3 Q]
    Summula

Vitus Kahl (d. 1735) [K3 Q]
    Commentaria supra libros Physicorum

Luke Haeller (d. 1739) [K3 Q]

Ceslao Stixa (d. 1740) [K3 Q]

Constanzo Lemmichen (d. 1740) [K3 Q]

Thomas Beran (d. 1742) [K3 Q]

Oswald Keller (d. 1742) [K3 Q]

France

James of St. Dominic (1616-1704) [Q]
   Defensio S. Thomae (Langres, 1667)
   Compendaria theologiae moralis explicatio
      (Paris, 1676)
   Ad concursum primae causae (Paris, 1679)

James Hyacinth Fejacq (1646-1715) [Q]
   Panegirique de S. Thomas (Toulouse, 1697)

James Lafon (1656-1715) [Q]
   Doctrina moralis de sacramentis
   Tractatus thomisticus moralis

Vincent van Severen (d. 1719) [Q]
   Theses sacrae (Louvain, 1700-01)
   Theologia de actibus humanis (Louvain, 1710)
   Theses theologicae (Louvain, 1718-19)

Anthony Cloche (1628-1720) [C3 Q]
   Comm. III (Rome, 1682)

Natalis Alexandre (1639-1720) [Q]
   Summa S. Thomae vindicata (Paris, 1675)
   Officium Sacramenti S. Thomae vindicatur
   Lettres aux Jesuites de la doctrine des
      Thomistes (1697)

Francis Mespolie (fl. 1720) [Q]
   Règlement de vie et des vertus (Paris, 1713)

Joseph Roux (fl. 1720) [Q]
   Sentiment de S. Thomas de l'aumone
      (Limoges, 1710)

Roman Martin (d. 1721) [Q]
   Tractatus de gratia divina

James Echard (1644-1724) [Q]
   S. Thomae Summa suo auctori vindicata
      (Paris, 1708)

Joseph Patin (d. 1725) [Q]
   Theologia moralis thomistica (Avignon, 1711)
   Theologia angelica

Bernard De Rabaudy (1651-1731) [Q]
   Exercitationes prolegomenorum theologiae
      (Toulouse, 1713)
   Comm. ST (Toulouse, 1713-15)

Giles Versmissen (1666-1731) [Q]
   Theses scripturisticae (Louvain, 1703)
   Theses theologicae (Louvain, 1712-29)
   Meditullium thomisticum (Antwerp, 1726)

Ignatius Hyacinth Amat de Graveson (1670-1733)
[M2 Q T]
   Tractatus de mysteriis et annis Christi
      (Rome, 1711)
   Comm. I-II (Rome, 1728-30)
   Epistolae apologeticae (Verona, 1737)

Henry Gautier (1698-1733) [Q]
   Philosophia universa (Louvain, 1729-31)

Augustine Everaert (1692-1738) [Q]
   Philosophia universa (Louvain, 1724)
   Theses sacrae (Louvain, 1731-32)

Hyacinth René Drouin (1680-1740) [Q R6]
   De re sacramentaria (1765)

                  Germany and Holland

Nicholas Cönen (d. 1713) [Q]
   Theses thomistico-canonico-civilistico-
      juridicae practicae (Coblenz, 1707)

Norbert Willemsen (1645-1716) [Q]
   Theses theologicae (Antwerp, 1679-82)

Raymond Nipels (1649-1716) [Q]
   Theses theologicae (Liège, 1690)

Ignatius Trainer (d. 1717) [Q]
   Hexicologia

Gaspar Vainque (d. 1719) [Q]
    Philosophia ad mentem Angelici (Louvain, 1718)

John Van den Busdom (d. 1721) [Q]
    Thomae Aquinatis de humanis actibus dogmata
        (Antwerp, 1710)
    Theses theologicae (Antwerp, 1715)

Bernard de Keyser (1651-1722) [Q]
    Sincera et interna vita (Bruges, 1703)

Hyacinth du Mont (1674-1723) [Q]
    Theses sacrae (Louvain, 1705)
    Verbum abbreviatum (Louvain)

Peter De Pape (d. 1724) [Q]
    Theses sacrae (Louvain, 1694)
    Theologia juris et justitiae (Louvain, 1711)

Raymond Hauben (d. 1725) [Q]
    Philosophia universa (Antwerp)

Raymond Massenaire (1645-1728) [Q]
    Philosophia universa (Louvain, 1693)

Peter Geeten (1672-1729) [Q]
    Theses sacrae (Louvain, 1714)
    Theses theologicae (Louvain, 1715-28)
    Theologia speculativa (Louvain, 1727)

Nicholas Schmidt (d. 1730) [Q]
    Theses theologicae (Luxembourg, 1726)

Gundisalvus De Hondt (d. 1731) [Q]
    Theses theologicae
        (Brussels 1692, Mechlin 1696, Louvain,
        1700-1702)

Gaspar Van Waerbeeck (d. 1731) [Q]
    Positiones scripturisticae (Antwerp, 1723)

Sebastian Knippenberg (1644-1733) [M2 Q]
    Opuscula (Cologne, 1700-21)
    Deus movens (Cologne, 1708)

Ambrose Van Huijsen (1673-1733) [Q]
    Theses theologicae (Antwerp, 1712-23)
    Theologia universa (Antwerp)

Benedict D´Estreé (1680-1735) [Q]
    Philosophia (Louvain, 1710)
    Theses sacrae (Louvain, 1720-21)

John Ferler (d. 1735) [Q]
    Columna philosophica

John Dursch (fl. 1736) [V2]
    Comm. II-II

Joseph Compas (1673-1737) [Q]
    Theses sacrae (1707)
    Theses theologicae (Louvain, 1729-32)
    Theologia speculativa (Louvain, 1731)
    Comm. I (Louvain, 1731)

John-Chrysostom Posteau (d. 1737) [Q]
    De justificatione (Brussels, 1687)
    De bonitate et malitia actuum humanorum
        (Brussels, 1687)
    De charitate (Brussels, 1687)
    De incarnatione (Brussels, 1687)
    Theses theologicae (Antwerp, 1704)

Constantine Herzog (fl. 1737) [V2]
    Comm. II-II, III

Matthew De Bie (1670-1738) [Q]
    Theses disputatoriae theologicae
        (Antwerp, 1722-23)
    Theses theologo-morales (Antwerp, 1724)
    Theses theologicae (Antwerp)
    Theologia (Antwerp, 1736)

Dominic De Wagheneerer (1699-1738) [Q]
    Theses philosophicae (Louvain, 1728-32)
    Theses sacrae (Louvain, 1736-37)

Ferdinand Grouwels (d. 1739) [Q]
    Theses theologicae (Mechlin, 1726)

Joseph Careeuw (d. 1739) [Q]
    Philosophia universa (Louvain, 1734)

Joseph Riedl (fl. 1749) [V2]
    Comm. III

Willibald Mohrenwalder (d. 1762) [M2]
    Comm. I (Ginsbergae, 1759)

Great Britain and Ireland

Christopher Connell (d. 1713) [Q]
    Theses theologicae de actibus humanis (Louvain)
    Theses theologicae de sacramentis
        (Louvain, 1709)

John O´Brien (d. 1713) [Q]
    Theses theologicae de incarnationis mysterio
        (Louvain, 1688)
    Theses theologicae de sacramenteis
        (Louvain, 1689)
    Theses theologicae de Deo (Louvain, 1690)

Christopher Frenz (fl. 1713) [Q]
    Comm. I

Edmund Burke (fl. 1713) [Q]
    De legibus, jure, justitia, et gratia
        (Louvain, 1703)
    Comm. I (Louvain, 1707)
    Comm. II, III (Louvain, 1708)

Michael MacQuilin (1659?-1714) [Q]
    Dissertatio de contritione (Paris, 1716)

John O´Heyn (1647-1715) [Q]
    Epilogus chronologicus Praedicatorum in regno
        Hyberniae (Louvain, 1706)

Michael MacEgan (d. 1715) [Q]
    Theses Theologicae (Louvain)

John Dillon (d. 1716) [Q]
    Theses theologicae (Louvain, 1700)

James Dillon (d. 1724) [Q]
    Theses theologicae de ultimo fine (Louvain)
    Theses theologicae de moralitate actuum
        humanorum (Louvain)
    Theses theologicae de Deo (Louvain)

Thomas Morley (d. 1724) [Q]
    Theses theologicae (Louvain)

Hyacinth Watson (d. 1724) [Q]
    Theses theologicae de homine (Louvain, 1723)
    Theses theologicae de virtutibus theologicis
        (Louvain, 1724)

Bonaventure Nagle (d. 1737) [Q]
    Evangelii secundum Matthaeum veritas
        (Louvain, 1735)

Italy

James Ricci (d. 1703) [Q]
    Instructio pro iis qui promovendi sunt ad
        ordines

John Benedict Perazzo (1631?-1705) [M2 Q]
    Thomisticus Ecclesiastes
        (Ferrara, 1692; Venice, 1700-1)

Ambrose Capello (1635?-1705) [Q]
    Sermones quadragesimales (Venice, 1691)

Thomas Mary Amendolia (fl. 1706) [R9]
    De poenitentia (Messana, 1687)
    Resolutiones morales (Naples, 1706)

Thomas Luccioni de Bonifacio (d. 1712) [Q W4]
    Veritatis moralis investigatio (Milan, 1702)
    Elucidarium vitae et operum D. Thomae
        (Genoa, 1705)

Dominic Ricci (d. 1712) [Q]
    Homo interior (Naples, 1709)
    Comm. ST (Naples, 1709-12)

Anthony Condomitti (d. 1712) [M2 Q R9]
    Comm. I-II (Naples, 1706-12)

Vincent Mary Ferri (d. 1714) [Q]
    Matthaeus scholasticus (Venice, 1702)

Michael Marinoni (d. 1714) [Q]
    Theses de locis theologicis (Naples, 1714)

Joseph Mary Tabaglio (d. 1714) [Q]
    Comm. ST

Paul Mary Canninus (d. 1716) [M2 Q]
    Cursus philosopho-metaphysicus
        (Bologna 1692, Milan 1692, Piacenza 1692-93)
    Comm. I. (Rome, 1709-17)

Paul-Mary Cauvinus (1642-1716) [Q]
    Cursus philometaphysicus
        (Bologna, Piacenza, 1692)
    Comm. I (Rome, 1709-1717)

Thomas-Mary Ferrari (1647-1716) Cardinal [Q]
    Opera philosophica
    Comm. I, II

Henry Saccardi (d. 1716) [Q]
    Tractatus philosophicus (Naples, 1716)

Augustine Bermingham (fl. 1713-17) [C]

Francis-Dominic Peratius (d. 1718) [Q]
    Theologicae veritates (Bologna, 1718)

Mario Diana (1645-1719) [Q]
    Idea jurium interioris fori (Palermo, 1705)

Basil Ferri (fl. 1719) [Q]
    S. Thomae elogium (Venice, 1696)

Edward Ambrose Burgis (fl. 1719) [Q]
    Prolegomena ad sacram scripturam
        (Louvain, 1716)

John Syri of Ovado (fl. 1720) [Q]
    Universa philosophia Aristotelico-thomistica
        (Venice, 1719)

Thomas-Mary Magliuolo (1660-1725) [Q]
    Tractatus de ordine supernaturali
    Tractatus de legibus
    Tractatus de justitia et jure

Thomas Pezzimenti (d. 1725) [Q]
    Scelta de morale (Palermo, 1725ff.)

Raphael Giocomazzi (d. 1725) [Q]
    Doctrina dogmatica (Venice, 1711)
    Radius moralis theologicus (Venice, 1724)

John-Mary Muti (1649-1727) [Q]
    Conclusiones thomisticae in primam partem

Albert-Mary Mammoliti (d. 1727) [Q R9]
    Philosophia

Pius-Thomas Masserotti (d. 1727) [Q]

Alexander Corradi (d. 1728) [C]

Gregory Selleri (1654-1729) [C3 Q]
    Propositiones damnatae (Rome, 1718-28)

Angelus-William Molo (1647-1737) [Q]
    Theses de locis theologicis (Bologna, 1701)

John-Dominic Siri (d. 1737) [Q]
    Universa philosophia (Venice, 1719)
    Universa thomistica theologia
        (Bologna, 1727-28)

Sylvester Martini (d. 1738) [C]

Vincent Passani (d. 1739) [Q]
    Alla gloria di S. Tommaso discorso
        (Cremona, 1709)

Vincent Louis Gotti (1644-1742) Cardinal [M2 W]
    Comm. ST (Bologna, 1727-35)

Hyacinth Maisano (d. 1743) [R9]
    Comm. ST
    Comm. in Aristotelis philosophiam

Pius Thomas Boeri (fl. 1745-69) [C]

Bernard Cimegotti (fl. 1762-69) [C]

Evenzio Martini (fl. 1767-69) [C]

Bernard Mary de Rubeis (Rossi) (1687-1775) [T W4]
    De gestis, scriptis, doctrina, S. Thomae
        (Venice, 1750)
    Opera omnia D. Thomae (Venice, 1745-88)
    Theologica summa (Paris, 1860)

Salvatore Mary Roselli (d. 1784) [H N2 T T2]
    Summa philosophica (Rome, 1777-83)

Augustine Chignoli (d. 1785) [C]

Dominic Crocenti [R9]
    Riflessioni cristiane (Messima, 1773)
    Meditazioni (Messina, 1794-90)

J. V. Patuzzi [T]
    Difesa della dottrina (Lucca, 1746)
    Lettere apologetiche (Venice, 1763)

D. Valfredi [T]
    De usu philosophiae (Genoa, 1777)

                        New World

Anthony De Torres (d. 1728) [Q]
    De gloriosissimo Ecclesiae doctore
        (Angelopoli, 1695)
    Philosophicae praelectiones

Ildephonse Gil (d. 1730) [Q]
    Cursus philosophiae

Hyacinth Anthony of Buenaventura (fl. 1759) [C6]
    Comm. I-II

John Barbosa (fl. 1767) [C6]

Bernaro Bazan [C6]
    Comm. I-II, III

Peter de Pravia [C6]
    De Eucharistia

Poland

John Damascene Lubienecki (fl. 1715) [Q]
    Inquisitio de gestis et miraculis B. Ceslai

Nicholas Oborski (d.1716) [Q]
    Conclusiones theologicae

Dominic Frydrychowicz (1645-1718) [Q]
    Manipulus theologicus ex prima parte
        (Cracow, 1691)

Angelus Wierzbowicz (d. 1731) [Q]
    Memoriale philosophiae (Danzig, 1702)

Spain

Charles de Bayona (fl. 1700) [Q]
    Lectiones

Jerome Matama (fl. 1700) [M2 Q]
    Comm. III

John Bolivar (fl. 1710) [Q]
    Thomisticae scholae controversiae
        (Salamanca, 1701)

Froylanus Diaz de Llanos (1648-1714) [Q]
    Philosophia naturalis (Complutum, 1691)
    Logica (Complutum, 1693)
    Brevis explicatio dialecticae (Madrid, 1694)
    De generatione et corruptione
        (Valladolid, 1699)

Peter Sanchez (1664-1719) [Q]
    Quodlibeta D. Thomas (Seville, 1718)

John de Montalvan (1661-1720) [M2 Q]
    Comm. I (Salamanca, 1729-31)

Joseph Gonzalez de Muñana (1679-1721) [Q]
    Dignitas philosophiae (Seville, 1702)
    Dignitas Aristotelis (Seville, 1702)

Seraphin Thomas Miguel (1651-1722) [Q]
    Comm. II-II

John Villalva (1669-1722) [Q]
    Cursus philosophici (Saragossa, 1715)
    Cursus theologici (Saragossa, 1717-19)

Dominic Perez (1661-1724) [M2 Q]
    Tractatus de incarnationis mysterio
        (Madrid, 1732)
    Tractatus de fide (Madrid, 1734)

Vincent Melis (d. 1724) [Q]
    Tractatus physicae

Joseph Bono (1657-1725) [Q]
    Comm. ST

Thomas de Granda (d. 1729) [Q]
    El sol de la verdad (Salamanca, 1729)

John of Aliaga (d. 1732) [M2 Q]
    Comm. I-II (Salamanca, 1726-32)

Michael Gosalbo (1680-1733) [Q]
    Vindictae Aquinaticae expositivae

Vincent Ferrer III (d. 1738) [Q]
    Epitome cursus theologici (Valencia, 1720-30)
    Opusculum theologicum de conscientia
        (Valencia, 1725)

Cajetan Benitez de Lugo (d. 1739) [M2]
    Comm. I-II (Rome, 1730-33)

John Thomas Boxadors (1703-80) Cardinal [H]
    Thomisticae doctrinae cultus (1757)

Anthony Michael Juranni [T]
    Pro commendatione S. Thomae (Madrid, 1789)

John Briz [T]
    Vida de S. Tomas (Madrid, 1748)

                    AUGUSTINIANS

Augustine Curtius (fl. 1700) [M2]
    Comm. I

Augustine Kneutgen (d. 1716) [M2]
   Comm. I-II (Brunn, 1702)

John Baptist Ininger (d. 1730) [M2]
   Comm. II-II (Monachii, 1797)
   Comm. III (Monachii, 1797)

Sigismund Buttner (fl. 1734) [M2]
   Comm. I

John de Contreras [C6]
   Comm. III

BENEDICTINES

Celestine Pley (d. 1710) [G]
   Theoremeta theologiae (Salzburg, 1711)

Louis Babenstuber (1660-1715) [W]
   Philosophia thomistica (Augsburg, 1706)
   Cursus theologiae moralis (Augsburg, 1718)

Placidus Renz sr. (d. 1730) [W]

Virgil Sedlmayr (d. 1732) [M2]
   Comm. III

Hyacinth Peri (d. 1733) [M2]
   Comm. I and I-II (Styrae, 1719-32)
   Comm. Supplementum

Henry Hardter (d. 1738) [M2]
   Comm. ST

Alphonse Wenzl (1660-1743) [M2 W]
   Comm. I, I-II, III

Placidus Renz jr. (d. 1748) [W]

Romanus Effinger (d. 1766) [M2 T]
   Comm. I-II (Constance, 1734)

Placidus Erkens [M2]
   Comm. I (Cologne, 1713)

CARMELITES

Sebastian of St. Joachim (d. 1714) [C7]
    Cursus theologiae moralis (1665-1724)

Angelo of St. Mary (b. 1715) [F3]

Henry of St. Ignatius (d. 1719) [M2]
    Comm. I-II (Louvain, 1713)

John of St. Michael (d. 1730) [M2]
    Comm. I (Seville, 1720)

Alphonse of the Angels (1663-1737) [C7]
    Cursus theologiae moralis (1665-1724)

Peter of the Conception [C6]

CISTERCIANS

Benedict Hueber [M2]
    Harmonia doctrinae S. Thomae et Thomistarum
        consona (Salem, 1718)

Raphael Koendig [M2]
    Harmonia doctrinae S. Thomae et Thomistarum
        consona (Salem, 1718)

JESUITS

G. Froelich (fl. 1703) [M2]
    Comm. III

Francis Wolker (1654-1714) [M2]
    Comm. III (Prague, 1705)

Peter Kirsch (1638-1721) [M2]
    Comm. I (Cologne, 1708)

Anthony Cordeyro (1641-1722) [F3 M2]
    Comm. ST

Christopher Rassler (d. 1723) [M2]
    Comm. I

J. B. Halden (1649-1726?) [M2]
    Comm. I

Francis Kolbe (1682-1727) [M2]
    Comm. St (Prague, 1740)

Bernard Jost (1669-1729) [M2]
    Comm. I, I-II, II-II

Beatus Amrhyn (1655-1731) [M2]
    Comm. I, I-II, III

Barthélemy des Bosses (1688-1738) [S6]

P. Pfister (d. 1743) [M2]
    De scholis thomistica et scotistica
        (Dillingen, 1708)

Nicholas Candela (fl. 1747) [A2]
    Cursus philosophicus

H. Postel (fl. 1758) [M2]
    Comm. III

Adrian Desruelles (1706-61) [M2]
    Comm. ST

Joseph Fitterer (fl. 1761) [M2]
    Doctrina selecta ex ST

J. Armand (fl. 1762) [M2]
    Comm. II-II (1762)

Gaspar Sagner (1720-81) [R]
    Institutiones philosophicae (Prague, 1755-58)

Emmanuel Azevedo [M2]
    Compendium ST

John Boursier [M2]
    Comm. III (Douai, 1734-35)

Peter of Ortigosa [C6]
    Comm. II-II
    De angelis
    De poenitentia

MINIMS

Francis Palanco (d. 1720) [M2]
    Comm. III (Madrid, 1706-31)

Joseph Mary Perrimezzi (d. 1740) [R9]
    De Deo (Naples, 1730-39)

VINCENTIANS AT PIACENZA

John Mary Pozzi (1702-75) [R]

John Dominic Cravosio (1725-76) [R]
    Psicologia

John Anthony Como (1739-92?) [R]
    Institutiones philosophicae

Bartholomew Bianchi (1761-1810?) [R]
    Institutiones philosophicae
    Metaphysica

Francis Grassi [R R8]
    Institutiones theologicae
    De anima

OTHERS

Armenia

Mechithar of Sebaste (1676-1749) [O]
    Translated ST into Armenian

John of Sebaste [O]
    Translated I into Armenian

Belgium

C. G. Daelman (d. 1731) [M2]
    Comm. ST (1746)

J. van Damme [T]
    Deus praedicandus (Louvain, 1706)

Paul Peter Vernaelde [T]
    Comm. III (Douai, 1734-35)

Colombia

Anthony Joseph Guzman (fl. 1753) [C6]
    De visione beatifica

Augustine Manuel de Alacon y Castro (fl. 1758)
[A2]
    Logica Parva

Rafael Mancera (fl. 1672) [C6]
    De anima

France

Appay [M2]
    Catena aurea theologiae Doctoris Angelici

Ferbos (Mercedarian) [M2]
    Comm. III

A. Touron [T]
    La vie de St. Thomas (Paris, 1737)

Germany and Austria

John Baptist Holzmann [T]
    Compendium vitae (Vienna, 1723)

Italy

John Baptist Comazzi (d. 1711) [H3 T]
    La coscienza (Trent, 1711)

John Claude Pozzobonello (Barnabite) (d. 1718)
[M2]
    Comm. ST (Milan, 1703-10)

Francis Mary Majo (Theatine) (d. 1726) [C]

Anthony Monici (fl. 1750) [C]
    De moralis theologiae principiis

Nicholas Antonelli (d. 1767) Cardinal [P P6]
    Specimen rationis in explanatione Summae
        (Rome, 1766)

John Baptist Crescenzi (1740-71) [C]
    Triplices de re theologica disputationes
        (Ferrera,1760)

Saint Alphonsus Liguori (Redemptorist) (1696-1787)
[W]
    Theologia moralis (1753-55)

Anthony Benadusi (fl. 1790) [C]
    Theologia dogmatico - scholastica

Thomas Capialbi (fl. 1790) [R9]
    Tractatus theologicus

Bartholomew Scardua (1733-1820?) [C]
    Lezioni di metafisica (Venice, 1776)

J. Santefelicius [T]
    Jansenii doctrina damnata (Naples, 1728)

Oct. Bucellani [T]
    Compendium vitae (Vienna, 1723)

P. M. Passerini [T]
    De hominum statibus (Rome, 1763-65)

                        Portugal

Estacio de Vargas (fl. 1731) [F3]
    Summaria totius philosophiae

Joseph Caetano (fl. 1747) [F3]
    Opinatio D. Thomae (Lisbon, 1747)
    Escola thomistica (Lisbon, 1749)

Russia

Hilarion Negrebetskii (fl. 1734) [R7]
    Theologica scholastica

Teofilatto Lopatinskii [R7]
    Scientia sacra

Spain

J. de Velasco [T]
    Vida de S. Tomás, tr. (Madrid, 1792)

Ph. Madalena [T]
    Crisis thomistica (Saragossa, 1719)

V. Calatayud [T]
    Mystica theologia (Valencia, 1754-56)

Valcarel [S6]

Nineteenth Century

DOMINICANS

France, Belgium, and Switzerland

Reginald Beaudoin [T]
   La prémotion physique (1879)

J. J. Berthier [H M2 T]
   L'étude de la Somme (1893)
   Tabulae Summae (Friburg, Switz., 1893)
   Sanctus Thomas Aquinas (Rome, 1914)

H. Bisschop [T]
   Thomistes et molinistes (Paris, 1897)

Thomas Bourard [J T]
   Philosophie (Paris, 1865)

M. D. Chapotin [T]
   L'ange de l'école (Arcis-sur-Aube, 1895)

Th. Coconnier [T T2]
   Panégyrique (Toulouse, 1888)
   Le vrai thomiste (1893)

H. M. Cormier [T]
   Etude sur St. Thomas (Toulouse, 1886)

A. M. Dummermuth (1841-1918) [M2 T T2]
   Republished Goudin's Tractatus theologici
      (Louvain, 1874)
   Doctrina praemotionis Paris, 1886)

Xavier Faucher [T]
   Summa theologica (Paris, 1887-89)

Hippolyte Gayrand [T]
    Le thomisme et le molinisme (Toulouse, 1889)
    Providence et libre arbitre (Toulouse, 1892)
    La prescience divine (1895)

H. Guillermin [T T2]
    La prémotion (1886)
    Le prédetérminisme (Paris, 1896)

H. M. Iweins [T]
    Les universités (Louvain, 1875)
    Saint Thomas (Louvain, 1880)

Jordan Jansen [T]
    De H. Thomas (Louvain, 1890)

Ch. A. Joyau [T]
    Saint Thomas (Poitiers, 1886)

Henry D. Lacordaire [T W5]
    Discours (Paris, 1852)

M. J. LaGrange [T]
    L'inspiration scripturaire (1895)

J. de Langen-Wendels [T]
    De l'instinct (Fribourg, 1897)

Lavy [M2 T]
    Conférences (Paris, 1884-88)
    Les anges (Paris, 1890)

Albert Lepidi (1838-1925) [A H T T2 W5]
    Elementa philosophiae christianae
        (Louvain, 1875)
    Cosmologia (Louvain, 1879)
    De ente generalissimo (Piacenza, 1881)

Ceslas Loyson [T]
    L'influence de St. Thomas (Albi, 1859)

V. Maumus [T T2]
    La doctrine spirituelle (Paris, 1885)
    La philosophie cartésienne (Paris, 1889)
    St. Thomas (Paris, 1890)
    Les doctrines politiques (1893)

Alexander Mercier [T]
    Le juste salaire (1896)

Andrew-Mary Meynard [T]
   La vie intérieure (Clermont-Ferrand, 1885)

A. Montagne [T T2]
   L'ésthetique (Toulouse, 1894)
   Origine de la société (1898-99)
   Les diverses formes de gouvernement (1900-02)

Mark de Munnynck [T]
   L'antomisme (Fribourg, 1898)

M. Ambrose Potton [T]
   Sentiments (Lyons, 1864)

M. B. Schwalm [T T2]
   Les récents progrès (1893)
   La propriété (1895)
   Le thomisme (1899)

A. Villard [T]
   La providence (1896-97)

              Germany, Austria, and Switzerland

Henry Seuse Denifle (1844-1905) [A T T2 W]
   Die Universitaten des Mittelalters bis 1400
      (Berlin, 1885)

Thomas Esser [T]
   Die Moglichkeiteiner anfangslosen Schopfung
      (Muenster, 1895)
   Questiones quodlibetales (1899)

Gundisalvus Feldner [M2 T T2]
   Der Einfluss Gottes (Graz, 1889)
   Das Verhaltnis der Wesenheit zu dem Dasein
      (1888-93)
   Die Neuthomisten (1894-96)

Ceslas M. Schneider [M2 S6 T T2]
   Natur, Vernunft, Gott (Regensburg, 1882)
   Das Wissen Gottes (Regensburg, 1884-86)
   Die sozialistische Staatsidee (Paderborn, 1894)

Great Britain

Pius Cavanagh [T]
   Life of St. Thomas (London, 1899)

Holland

C. Van den Berg [T]
   De ideis divinis (S'Hertogenbosch, 1872)
   Beatissima Virgo (S'Hertogenbosch, 1874)

J. Van de Groot (S6 T T2]
   De philosophia S. Thomae (1890-91)
   St. Thomas philosophe (1894)

Italy

Louis Albini [T]
   Dissertazione polemica (Rome, 1817)

Augustine Bausa (fl. 1881) Cardinal [P5]

R. Bianchi [T]
   De constitutione monarchica ecclesiae
      (Rome, 1870)

L. Buonpensiere (d. 1929) [F M2 T]
   Comm. III (Rome, 1899)
   De Deo uno (Rome, 1901)

Dominic Burzio [R9]

Paul Carbo [D2 H W5]

M. Cicognani [T]
   Sulla vita e sulle opere (Venice, 1874)
   La Eucharistia (Rome, 1898)

R. Cocoz [T]
   Orazione (Florence, 1865)
   Omaggio (Prato, 1874)

Hyacinth de Ferrari (1805-74) [N W5]
   Philosophia thomistica (Rome, 1851)

Pius Albert del Corona [T W5]
   I cardini della felicità (Florence, 1876)
   I misteri de Gesù (San Miniato, 1882)
   La piccola Somma (Florence, 1889-92)

Norbert del Prado [T]
   Panegirico (Manila, 1889)

Vincent Gatti (1811-82) [P5 W2]
   Institutiones apologeticae (1866)

Francis Gaude (d. 1860) Cardinal [P P5]

Dominic Mary Gaudenzi (1831-84) [C]
   Della sede dell'anima (1881)
   S. Tommaso e la scienza (1881)

Thomas Gaudenzi (d. 1884) [S6 T]
   La scienza (Bologna, 1874)

Thomas Mary Granello (1840-1911) [C T]

Vincent Joseph Lombardo (1836-1909) [C]
   Compendium SCG

Jerome M. Mancini [T]
   Elementa philosophica (Rome, 1898)

Vincent Fortunato Marchese [T]
   S. Tommaso (Perugia, 1839)
   Onoranze all'angelico dottore (Genoa, 1874)
   Delle benemerenze di S. Tommaso (Genoa, 1874)

Giles Mauri [T]
   Orazione panegirica (Rieti, 1882)

A. Reali [T]
   L'infallibità (Rome, 1870)

D. P. Rossi [T W5]
   Influenza di S. Tommaso (Venice, 1874)

Hyacinth B. Rossi (1826-99) [W5]
   Spiritualità dell'anima umana (1876)

T. M. Salzano [T]
   Vie de St. Thomas (Paris, 1883)

Joseph Sanvito [T]
   Il sesto centenario (Rome, 1874)

Vincent Schembri [T]
    S. Tommaso (Malta, 1874)

M. Spada [T]
    Il peccato originale (Naples, 1839)

John Talia (d. 1843) [R9]
    Saggio di Estetica (Venice, 1822)
    Elementa theologiae (Naples, 1827)

John Thomas Tosa (d. 1892) [P]
    De sacramentis

Vincent Vera [R9]

Zanecchia [T]
    Inspiratio scripturarum (Rome, 1899)

Thomas M. Zigliara (1833-93) Cardinal
[F N P T W2 W5]
    Della luce intellettuale (Rome, 1874)
    Commentaria S. Thomae (1876)
    Summa philosophica (Lyons and Paris, 1887)

                    Philippines

Joachim Fonseca [T]
    Panegirico (Manila, 1865)

                    Portugal

Joseph Vidal (fl. 1827) [H W5]
    Origin of the Revolutionary Errors of Europe

                    Spain

Francis Alvarado (1756-1814) [H T2 W5]
    Cartas filosoficas (Madrid, 1825)

P. Alvarez [T]
    Religion (Barcelona, 1890)

E. F. Arias [T]
   Santo Tomás (Manila, 1894)
   Panegirico (Madrid, 1902)

J. Buitrago [T]
   Armonia entre la fé y la razon (Valencia, 1895)

Thomas Lorente e Ibanez [T]
   Discurso (Valencia, 1895)

J. M. Moran [T]
   Teologia moral (Madrid, 1883)

Pascual (d. 1856) [W2 W5]

Raphael Puigcerver (fl. 1826) [H T T2]
   Philosophia Thomae Aquinatis (Valencia, 1820)

Anthony Sendil [H]
   De vera ac salubri philosophia
      (Gerona, 1852-53)

Zefrino Gonzalez y Diás Tuñon (1831-94) Cardinal
[H T W5]
   Estudios sobre la filosofia de Santo Tomas
      (Manila, 1864)
   Philosophia elementaria (Madrid, 1868)
   Estudios religiosos, filosoficos, cientificos,
      y sociales (Madrid, 1873)
   Historia de la filosofia (Madrid, 1878)

                United States and Canada

Th. Aug. Dyson [T]
   The life of the Angelic Doctor (New York, 1881)

L. F. Kearney [T T2]
   The Existence of God (1891)
   What we Owe to the Summa (1893)

Edward Gregory Lawrence van Becellaere [M]
   La philosophie en Amérique (New York, 1904)

Unknown Country

L. J. Hickey [T]
   Le principe du "laissez faire"
      (Fribourg i. S., 1897)

BROTHERS OF THE CHRISTIAN SCHOOLS

Brother Barbas [T2]
   St. Thomas´s Latest Critic (1885)

Albert Bruny (Brother Louis de Poissy) (1835-1922)
[J]
   Cours élémentaire de philosophie (1875)

Joseph J. Conlon (Brother Chrysostom) [M S6 T]
   The Theistic Argument (1894)
   Elementa philosophiae (New York, 1897)

Patrick Francis Mullany (Brother Azarias)
(1847-93) [S6 T2]
   Essays Philosophical (Chicago, 1896)

CAPUCHINS

Joseph of Leonessa [T]
   L´Immaculée Conception (1896)
   Des Areopagiten Buch (1900)

Joseph Calasanctius Vives y Tutó (1854-1913)
Cardinal [M2]
   Summula Summae (published)

JESUITS

Belgium

Aug. Castelein [T2]
   Cours de philosophie (Namur, 1887-89)
   Psychologie (Namur, 1890)
   Le socialisme (Brussels, 1896)

Louis de San (d. 1904) [T T2]
   Institutiones metaphysicae (Louvain, 1881)
   De Deo uno (Louvain, 1894)

Gustave Lahousse [T T2]
   Praelectiones metaphysicae (Louvain, 1888)
   Summa philosophica (Louvain, 1892)

John Van der Aa [S6 T2]
   Philosophiae conspectus (Louvain, 1886)

A. Vermeersch [T]
   Universa theologia scolastica (Bruges, 1900-03)

                        Chile

Francis Ginebra [S6 T2]
   Elementos de filosofía
      (Santiago de Chile, 1887)
   Elementos de Etica (Santiago de Chile, 1889)

                        England

Bernard Boedder [T2]
   Natural Theology (1891)

Richard F. Clarke [T2 W]
   The Existence of God (New York, 1887)

Thomas Harper (1821-93) [T2]
   Evidence and Certainty (Manchester, 1876)
   Metaphysics of the Schools (London, 1879-84)

Joseph Rickaby (1845-1932) [A T2 W2]
   Aquinas Ethicus (New York, 1892)
   Summa contra gentiles (1905)

                 France and Switzerland

Louis Billot (1846-1931) Cardinal [H M2 T]
   De Verbo Incarnato (Rome, 1892)
   De Deo uno et trino (Rome, 1893)

Carbonelle [T2]
    La science et la philosophie (Paris, 1881)

Theodore de Régnon [T T2]
    Métaphysique de causes (Paris, 1885)

H. Ramière [T T2]
    La composition des corps (Paris, 1877)

F. Rothenflue [T2]
    Institutiones philosophiae
        (Lyons, Paris, 1846-52)

                    Germany and Switzerland

J. Biederlack [T]
    Zur Gesellschafts- und Wirthschaftslehre (1896)

B. Felchlin [T]
    Lehre des hl. Thomas (1892)

Joseph Kleutgen (1811-83) [H S T T2]
    Die Theologie der Vorzeit (Muenster, 1853-60)
    Die Philosophie der Vorzeit (Muenster, 1860-63)

Limburg [T]
    Sebszeichnung der Gnadenlehre (1877)
    Die Gnadenlehre (1877)

Theodore Meyer [T]
    Institutiones juris naturalis
        (Freiburg i. B., 1885)

Jul. Muellendorf [T]
    Die Hinordnung der Werke auf Gott (1885)
    Die ubernaturliche Motio (1893)

J. Mueller [T]
    St. Thomas und die moderne Wissenschaft
        (Munich, 1894)
    Der Gottesbeweis aus der Bewegung (1897)

G. Patiss [T]
    Das leiden Jesu (Regensburg, 1883)
    Die Geheimnisse unseres Herrn (Innsbruck, 1896)

T. Pesch [A T]
  Institutiones philosophiae naturalis
    (Freiburg i. B., 1880)
  Institutiones psychologicae
    (Freiburg i. B.,1896-98)

                    Italy

Francis Altini (1839-84) [D]
  Etica

Gioacchino Ambrosini (b. 1857) [D]
  Logica
  Metafisica
  Theologia naturalis

Titus Bottagisio (1851-1932) [D]
  Etica

John Mary Cornoldi (1822-92) [C D H T]
  Lezioni di filosofia (1872)
  La reforma filosofica (Bologna, 1880)
  Il sistema fisico (1891)

Charles Mary Curci (1810-91) [H]
  Memoirs (Florence, 1891)

Michael de Maria (1836-1913) [A H S T]
  Opuscula (Città di Castello, 1886)
  Philosophia peripatetico-scholastica
    (Rome, 1892)

Pius De Mandato [F S6 T]
  Philosophicae institutiones (Rome, 1894)
  Le specie organiche (Rome, 1895)

P. Freddi [T]
  Gesù Cristo (Rome, 1898)

Matthew Liberatore (1810-92) [T]
  Institutiones philosophicae (Naples, 1840)
  Della conoscenza intellettuale (Rome, 1858)

John Mai (1819-98) [D]
  Logica
  Metaphysica
  Teodicea

Guy Mattiussi (1852-1925) [D D2]
    Principi di filosofia (Milan, 1895)
    Distinzione tra essenza ed esistenza
        (Florence, 1911)
    La philosophie de St. Thomas (Turin, 1926)

Joseph Mauri (1849-1923) [D D2]
    De Deo
    Quaestiones logicae et metaphysicae

Camille Mazella [T]
    Conscenza intellettiva (1885)

Felix Pignataro (d. 1905) [M2]
    Comm. I, I-II

Vincent Remer (1843-1910) [F H S6]
    Summa philosophiae scholasticae (Prati, 1895)

Santo Schiffini (1841-1906) [H R9 T]
    Principia philosophica (Turin, 1886)
    Institutiones philosophicae (Turin, 1889)

Francis Salis Seewis (1835-98) [S6 T2]
    Della conoscenza sensitiva (Prato, 1881)

Dominic Sordi (1790-1880) [H]

Serafino Sordi (1793-1865) [D D2 N]
    De studio theologiae in nostra societate
        (Rome, 1854)
    Ontologia (Milan, 1940)
    Theologia naturalis (Milan, 1945)

Louis Taparelli d'Azeglio (1793-1864) [D2 H T T2]
    Della sovranità del popolo (Florence, 1849)
    Corso elementare di natural diritto
        (Naples, 1857)
    Le ragioni del bello (Rome, 1860)

Julius Trabucci (1863-1907) [D]
    Quaestioni filosofiche

                        Poland

Anthony Langner (1833-1902) [S2]
    Sw. Tomasz i dzisiejsza filozofia (1884)
    Projecie o Bogu (1884-85)

Portugal

Francis Xavier Rondina (1827-97) [T2]
   Compendio de philosophia (Macao, 1869-70)

Spain

John Andrullo [T]
   El estado esta subordinado (1880)

S. Mendine [T2]
   Curso de filosofía (Madrid, 1886)
   Institutiones philosophiae
      (Valladolid, Cuenta, 1886-88)

John Joseph Urráburu [H S6 T2]
   Institutiones philosophicae (Valladolid, 1890)

United States

James Conway (1849-1905) [S6 M]
   Christian Ethics

Charles Coppens [S6 T2]
   Moral Philosophy (New York, 1896)

Aemilius de Augustinis [S6]
   De Deo uno (1884)

Walter H. Hill (1822-1907) [M S6]
   Elements of Philosophy (Baltimore, 1873)
   Ethics (Baltimore, 1878)

Louis Jouin (1818-99) [S6 T2]
   Praelectiones de iure naturali (1860-61)
   Elementa philosophiae moralis (1865)
   The Study of Philosophy (1869)

John J. Ming [S6 T2]
   The Existence of God (1881-82)
   The Data of Modern Ethics (New York, 1894)

William Poland (b. 1848) [M S6 T2]
    Fundamental Ethics (Boston, 1894)
    Rational Philosophy (New York, 1896)

Maurice Ronayne (1828-1903) [S6 T2]
    Religion and Science (New York, 1879)

Nicholas Russo (1845-1902) [S6 T W2]
    De homine (Woodstock, 1882)
    Summa philosophica (Boston, 1885)

Blase Schiffini (1839-1913) [R9 T T2 W2]
    De motu hominis in Deum (Woodstock, 1888)

                        MARISTS

Bulliot [S6]
    La théorie des catégoires (1897)

E. Peillaube [A S6]
    Théorie des Concepts (Paris, 1895)

                      PASSIONISTS

Blessed Dominic Barberi (d. 1849) [P]
    L'azione diviina sulla libertà umana
        (Rome, 1966)

Giacomo Sperati (d. 1886) [P]

Sylvester Zannelli (d. 1879) [P]

                      SULPICIANS

P. M. Brin (1843-94) [S6]
    De intellectualismo

Gabriel Bulliat [T T2]
    Thesaurus philosophiae thomisticae
        (Nantes, 1899)

Albert Farges [A S6 T2]
  L'objectivité de la perception (Paris, 1885)
  Matière et forme (Paris, 1888)
  La vie (Paris, 1892)

Paul Vallet [T T2]
  Praelectiones philosophicae (Paris, 1879)
  Le beau (Paris, 1883)

VINCENTIANS AT PIACENZA

Carl Alliora [R]
  Tractatus theologici

A. Alvigni [R]
  Quaesita circa philosophiam

Albert Barberis (1847-96) [R S6 T T2]
  Positivismus (1887)
  Esse formale estne rei intrinsecum an non
    (Piacenza, 1887)

Vincent Fioruzzi (1785-1832) [R R8]
  Institutiones philosophicae

Joseph Lusardi (fl. 1814) [R]
  Adnotationes philosophicae

Anthony Mantenga (1759-1811) [R]
  Institutiones philosophicae

Joseph Mary Martinengo (1748-1836) [R]
  Christiana philosophia

Francis De Mattias (fl. 1870) [R]
  Institutiones philosophicae

Andrew Rossi (1772-1817) [R]
  Adnotationes philosophicae

Cajetan Salvi (fl. 1841-47) [R]
  Cursus philosophiae

OTHERS

Belgium

S. Deploige [T2]
    La propriété (Louvain, 1895)

Désiré Joseph Mercier (1851-1926) [A T2]
    La philosophie de S. Thomas (1882)
    Le déterminisme (Louvain, 1883-84)
    La philosophie néo-scolastique (1894)

D. Nys [T2]
    Le problème cosmologique (Louvain, 1888)
    La notion du temps (Louvain, 1898)

Bohemia

Havaty [S6 T]
    Die Philosophie des hl. Thomas von Aquino
    (1885)

Eugene Kaderavek [S6 T]
    Aristotelisch-thomistischen Philosophie (1890)
    Psychologie (1894)

Pospisil [S6 T]
    Philosophie (1885)

Vychodil [S6]
    Die Existenz Gottes (1889)

Colombia

Rafael Mary Carrasquilla (b. 1857) [C4 S6]
    El estudio de la filosofia (1881)
    Essai sur la doctrine libérale (1895)

Joseph Eusebius Caro (1817-53) [S6 T2]

Michael Anthony Caro (b. 1843) [A2 C4 S6 T2]
    El utilitarismo (Bogotá, 1869)

Richard de la Para [S6 T2]

Mallarino [S6 T2]

Margallo [S6 T2]

Luis Maria Mora [A2]
    Apuntes sobre Balmes (1897)

Joaquin Mosquera [S6 T2]

Joaquín Gomez Otero (1848-1919) [A2 C6]
    Philosophiae definitiones (Bogatá, 1918)

Samuel Ramirez Arbeláez [A2]
    La filosofia positivista (1898)

Gabriel Rosas [C4]

Mario Valenzuela [S6 T2]
    El principio de utilidad (Bogotá, 1857)

Philip de Vergara y Caycedo (1745-1818) [A2]
    Filosofía natural
    Filosofos griegos

                    Eastern Europe

J. Domaszewicz [T]
    Swiati czlowiek (Warsaw, 1899)

P. A. Gornisiewicz [T]
    Pro dogmate infallibilitatis (1894-96)

Silvester Malevanskii (d. 1908) [R7]

Peter Pazmany, Cardinal [T]
    Theologia scholastica (Budapest, 1899-1901)

R. Tersch [T]
    Meditationen (Prague, 1885-86)

J. Zmavc [T]
    Die Werththeorie (1899)
    Die Prinzipien der Moral (1899)

France, Belgium, and Switzerland

George-Henry Bach [J T]
    De philosophia morali (Rouen, 1836)

M. Bach [T]
    De l´état de l´âme (Rouen, 1835)

Bainvel [T]
    L´idée de l´église (1899)

U. Baltus [T]
    Une apologie protestante (1898)

Abbé Bandel [J T]
    Opuscules (Paris, 1856-58)

Abbé Banet [T]
    L´adorable sacrement (Paris, 1854)

John-Francis Bareille [J T]
    Histoire de St. Thomas (Paris, 1846)

L. Barnard [T]
    Quid utilitatis (1879)

Ch. Barret [J T]
    Etudes philosophiques (Paris, 1848)

Bartin [W5]

L. Baudier [T]
    La prédétermination (1887)

Alb. Bazaillas [T]
    De regimine principum (Montauban, 1892)

Beney [W5]

M. S. Berthier [M2]
    Comm. I, III (Turin, 1899-1900)

Besson [T]
    Panégyrique (Toulouse,1881)

L. Birot [T]
    Panégyrique (1897)

Abbé Bluteau [T]
    Cathéchisme catholique (Paris, 1865)

Louis Boitel [T]
    St. Thomas (Lille, 1895)

A. Bonnetty [T]
    L'origine de nos connaissances (1846-47)

L. Bordes [T]
    Summae theologiae minutio (Paris, 1849)

T. Boulas [T]
    De regimine principum (Bar-le-Duc, 1880)

L. C. Bourquard [J T]
    De la connaissance (Besancon, 1877)
    De l'esthétique (1899-91)

L. Boursin [T]
    Les sermons (Paris, 1882)

M. de Boylesve [T]
    St. Thomas (Paris, 1886)

G. Bressoles [T]
    Les lois (Toulouse, 1853)

N. Cacheux [J T W5]
    La philosophie (Paris, 1858)

P. Carbonel [T]
    Excerpta philosophica (Paris etc., 1882)

Peter John Carle [J T]
    La vie et les écrits (Paris, 1846)

Justinian Carmagnolle [J T]
    La Somme théologique (Draguignan, 1860 ff.)

E.-M. Caro [T]
    La philosophie (1858)

Lawrence Caron [T]
   La perception (Amiens,1894)

M. Casalis [T]
   La question sociale (Montauban, 1901)

Chareyre (Marist) [A]

Chastellain [T]
   La Somme (1887)

Chicco [F]

J. A. Chollet [T]
   St. Thomas a l´université d´Amsterdam (1897)
   De la connaissance (1898)
   La notion de l´ordre (Paris)

A. Chretien [T]
   Le mouvement néo-thomiste (1899)

M. Coignard [T]
   Bossuet et St. Thomas (Angers, 1885)

Emile Combes [J T]
   La psychologie (Montpellier, 1860)

G. Contestin [T]
   Le sixième centenaire (1874)

Cosson [T]
   L´ange de l´Ecole (Coutances, 1884)

Edward Crahay [T]
   La politique (Louvain, 1896)

L. Crolet [T T2]
   Doctrine philosophique (Paris, 1890)

P. Dadolle [T]
   Panégyrique (1889)

F. V. Danton [T]
   Les passions (Limé, 1895)

A. Dard [T]
   La théodicée (Paris, 1892)

Stephen Darley [T]
   La volonté libre (1899)
   La liberté (1900)

Abbé Daurelle [T]
   Les événements de Fontet (Rome,1878)

Barbey d´Aurevilly [T]
   Saint Thomas (Paris, 1862)

David [T W5]
   La philosophie (1859)

Edgar de Bruyne [M4]
   Saint Thomas d´Aquin

J. de Coster [T]
   La finalité (Louvain, 1887)

Mme. de Desmousseaux de Givré [T]
   Vie de St. Thomas (Paris, 1888)

De Genoude [M2]
   Questions from ST

J. de Kernaeret [T]
   Le bible et la somme (1881)

D. Delaunay [J T T2]
   De origine idearum (Paris, 1876)

R. de Liechty [T T2]
   L´être et l´essence (Bar-le-Duc, 1883)

Amédée de Margerie [S6]

Vincent De Pascal [T2]
   Saint Thomas (Poitiers, 1878)

Charles de Rémusat [J T W]
   La philosophie (1857)

Louis de Rue [T]
   Le culte et les reliques (Lille, 1880)

Desprez [T]
   Panégyrique (1882)

Abbé D´hulst (1841-96) [J T T2 W5]
    Mélanges philosophiques (1892)
    Nouveaux mélanges philosophiques (Paris, 1909)

Jules Didiot [T T2]
    St. Thomas (Paris, 1874)
    Les actes du pape Léon (1880-81)
    Saint Thomas, est-il socialiste? (Paris, 1900)

Edmund Domet de Vorges (1829-1910) [A J T T2]
    La perception (Paris, 1892)
    Les certitudes (Fribourg, 1897)

Claude Joseph Drioux [J M2 T]
    La Somme théologique (Paris, 1851-54)

Th. Duboscq [T]
    Les émotions (Paris, 1896)

A. Dupeyrat [T T2]
    Manductio ad scholasticam (Paris, 1884)

A. Dupont [T T2]
    Thèses métaphysiques (Louvain, 1875)
    La prédétermination (1882-84)
    Spiritualité de l´âme (Lyons, 1885)

E. Germer Durand [T]
    Summa philosophica (Paris, 1853)

Peter-Francis Ecalle [J]
    Somme contre les Gentils (1854-57)

V. Ermoni (d. 1910) [H3 T]
    La psychologie experimentale (1898)

Farjou [T]
    Panégyrique (Toulouse, 1897)

Henry Robert Feugueray [F2 J T]
    Les doctrines politiques (Paris, 1857)

George Fonsegrive [T2]
    Le libre arbitre (Paris, 1887)
    La causalité efficiente (Paris, 1893)

C. Fontaine [T]
    De la sensation (Louvain, 1885)

Abbé Fournet [J T]
   Opuscules (Paris, 1856-58)

Frédault (d. 1895) [F2]
   Traité d´anthropologie (1863)
   Forme et matière (Paris, 1876)

Stanislaus Fretté [T]
   Summa contra gentiles (Paris, 1874)
   Summa theologica (Paris, 1882)

Bartholomew Froget [T]
   Le Saint Esprit (Paris, 1896)

P. Garaud [T]
   Panégyrique (Toulouse, 1894)
   Panégyrique (Toulouse, 1898)

Joseph Gardair [A J S6 T T2]
   Corps et âme (Paris, 1892)
   Philosophie de St. Thomas (Paris, 1895)

Gerardin [T]
   La fin des temps (Paris, 1885)

Mgr. Germain [T]
   Panégyrique (Toulouse, 1891)

P. Goux [T]
   De sermonibus (Paris, 1856)

Eugene Grand-Claude [J W5]
   Breviarium philosophiae (1863)

Grandelande [F]

Gratry [J]
   De la connaissance de Dieu (1853)

J. Hunnaeus [T]
   Summae theologiae conclusiones (Paris, 1890)

Theophilus Irneh [T]
   Saint Thomas (Lille, 1880)

Jaccoud [T]
   La science moderne (1884)

Charles B. Jourdain (1817-86) [F2 J M4 T T2]
    La philosophie de S. Thomas d´Aquin
        (Paris, 1858)

F. Lachat [J M2 T]
    La Somme théologique (Paris, 1854)

Mayeul Lamey [T]
    La philosophie (Pau, 1883)

Mgr. Tenet LaMothe [T]
    Panégyrique (Toulouse, 1881)

Mgr. Landriot [T]
    St. Thomas (Paris, 1864)

Frederick Lebrethon [J M2 P T]
    Petite Somme théologique (Paris, 1861-63)
    Summa minor (Paris, 1872)

Henry Lecoultre [T]
    La psychologie (Lausanne, 1883)

E. C. Lesserteur [T T2]
    Le thomisme (Paris, 1883)
    La prédestination (Paris, 1888)

Charles Lévêque (1818-1900) [J]

L. Maisonneuve [T]
    Panégyrique (Toulouse, 1898)

G. Malé [M2 T]
    La théologie de St. Thomas (Paris, 1857)

P. Mannens [T]
    De praedestinatione (Louvain, 1883)

P. Maré [T]
    Summa theologica (Paris, 1882)

Claude-Francis Maréchal [J T]
    De legis natura (Lyons, 1854)

E. Marquigny [T]
    Le centenaire (1874)

F. Million [T]
    La composition substantielle des corps
        (Paris, 1897)

H. Monnier [T]
    La foi (Paris, 1893)

J. Monsabré [T W5]
    Panégyrique (Toulouse, 1893)

Leo Montet [J T W5]
    Mémoire sur Saint Thomas (Paris, 1847)
    Ethica (Paris, 1848)

A. Murgue [T]
    Ontologie (Lyons, 1876)

L. Nadeau [T]
    De regimine principum (Paris, 1871)

E. Naville [T W5]
    L'oeuvre de St. Thomas (Paris, 1859)

Aug. Onclair [T]
    Le droit (1890)

Pages [T]
    Panégyrique (Verdun, 1891)

Ad. Aloysius Paquet [M2]
    Comm. ST (2nd ed., c. 1900)

Charles Passero de Corneliano [T W5]
    Les principes politiques (Paris, 1819)

Abbé Péronne [T]
    Panégyrique (Paris, 1867)
    Chaine d'Or (Paris, 1868)

E. Pesnelle [T]
    L'autorité scientifique (1882)

H. Philibert [T]
    La vie (Paris, 1885)

Clodius Piat [S6 T]
    Nostrae ideae (Paris, 1890)
    La liberté (Paris, 1894-95)

Francis Picavet [T T2]
    Le mouvement néo-thomiste (1892)

A. Pillet [T]
    Oratio panegyrica (Arras, 1881)
    Oratio (1899)

Poulain [T]
    Examen de la doctrine (Dieppe, 1883)

P. H. Prosper [T]
    La prédétermination (Paris etc., 1883)
    La Somme theologique (Lierre, 1894)

H. R. Quilliet [T]
    Doctrina socialis (1894)

R. P. Ramey [T]
    L'infini (1886)

M. J. Raynal [T]
    Panégyrique (Toulouse, 1889)

O. Rey [T]
    Etudes de biologie (1883)

Jerome Ribet [M2]
    La clef de la Somme théologique (1883)

Car. Rohart [T]
    Oratio (Ambiani, 1895)

Michael Rosset [J T T2 W5]
    Philosophia catholica (Paris, 1866)

F. A. Roullet de la Bouillerie [P4 T]
    L'homme (Paris, 1880)
    Il verbo (1882)
    Panégyrique (Bordeaux,1882)

Peter Celestine Roux-Lavergne (1802-74)
[J S T V W5]
    Republished Goudin's Philosophia (Paris, 1851)
    Compendium philosophiae (1856)
    Summa philosophica (Paris, 1861)

Henry Sauvé [P T]
    Le sixième centenaire (Amiens, 1875)
    Verités (Paris, 1888)

Ch. Secretan [T]
    La restauration du thomisme (1884)

J. B. Terrien [T]
   De unione hypostatica (Paris, 1894)

A. Thiery [T]
   Les beaux-arts (Louvain, 1896)

Thomas of Jesus (Passionist) [T]
   Le Saint Esprit (La Trappe, 1896)

Thuault [P]

G. C. Ubags [T]
   Métaphysique (1866)

Canon Valentin [T]
   Panégyrique (Toulouse, 1899)

G. van den Gheyn [T]
   La religion (1891)

A. Van Weddingen [P5 S6]
   La philosophie critique (Brussels, 1889)

Abbé Vedrine [J T]
   Opuscules (Paris, 1856-58)

Gioacchino Ventura de Raulica (Theatine)
(d. 1861) [F2 N P P5 S6 T2 W W5]
   De methodo philosophandi (1828)
   La raison philosophique et la raison catholique
      (1851)
   La philosophie chrétienne (Paris, 1861)

E. D. Ysalquier [T]
   Summa philosophica (Paris, 1853)

          Germany, Austria, Switzerland

Fr. Abert [T]
   Die Einheit des Seins in Christo
      (Regensburg, 1889)
   Compendium theologiae (Wurzburg, 1895)

Ackermann [T]
   Freiheit bei St. Thomas (c. 1891)

Aurelius Adeodatus [T]
    Die Philosophie der Neuzeit (Cologne, 1887)
    Cardinals Jos. Pecci Schrift (Mainz, 1888)

Basil Antoniades [T]
    Die Staatslehre (Leipzig, 1890)

J. J. Baumann [T W5]
    Die Staatslehre (Leipzig, 1873)
    Thomas von Aquino (Munich,1874)

W. Benzler [T]
    Ueber den hl. Thomas (1872)

P. J. Boecker [T]
    De statu justitiae originalis (Cologne, 1868)

C. A. Bosone [T]
    Der Kenntnis der Staatsphilosophie (Bonn, 1894)

J. Brookhoff [T]
    Die Erkennbarkeit Gottes (1887-91)

Francis James Clemens (1815-62) [H P S T]
    De scholasticorum sententia philosophiam esse
        theologiae ancillam (Muenster, 1856)

Ernest Commer (1847-1928) [A T W2]
    Die Thomistische Lehre von Weltfange (1883)
    System der Philosophie (Muenster, 1883-85)

Henry Contzen [T]
    De oeconomica politica (Basel, 1861)
    Die Staatslehre (Cassel, 1870)

A. Daniels [T]
    St. Thomas (1897)

John Delitzsch [T]
    Die Gotteslehre (Leipzig, 1870)

B. Doerholt [T]
    De Veritate (1896)

B. Duhr [T]
    Die Erlaubtheit des Tyrannenmordes (1893)

W. Ph. Englert [M2 T]
    Von der gnade Christi (Bonn, 1896)

R. Eucken [T]
    Thomas als Philosoph (1882)
    Die Philosophie (Halle, 1886)
    Frohschammers Thomas (1890)

J. Frohschammer (1821-93) [T]
    Die Theologie des Thomas (Leipzig, 1889)
    Die Philosophie des Thomas (Leipzig, 1889)

J. Geyser [T]
    Die Warhnehmung des Aussenwelt (1899)

Michael Glossner (1837-1909) [M2 T]
    Die Gnade (Mainz, 1871)
    Der Prinzip der Individuation (Paderborn, 1888)
    Die Philosophie des hl. Thomas (1895)

F. Göttig [T]
    Die Tugendlehre (Kiel, 1840)

B. H. Grundkotter [T]
    Der christlichen Vollkommonheit
        (Regensburg, 1887)

Constantin Gutberlet [A T2]
    Founder of Philosophisches Jahrbuch
    Lehrbuch der Philosophie (Muenster, 1890)
    Thomas von Aquin (1893)

F. Hettinger [T]
    Die europäische Civilisation (Frankfurt, 1880)

H. Hoertel [T]
    Thomas von Aquino (Augsburg, 1846)

H. Holtzmann [T]
    Die Scholastik (Karlsruhe, 1874)

Joseph Hontheim [T]
    Institutiones theodicae (Freiburg i. Br., 1893)

S. Huber [T]
    Die Glückseligkeitslehre (Freising, 1893)

H. Hurter [T]
    Sermones (Innsbruck, 1874)
    Das Dogma der unbeflekten Empfängnis (1893)

Lawrence Janssens (Benedictine) [M2]
    Comm. ST (Freiburg i. B., 1899 ff.)

A. Kastil [T]
    Erkenntnis des Guten (Vienna, 1900)

Nicholas Kaufmann [S T T2]
    Die Existenz eines Ersten Bewegers
        (Lucerne, 1882)
    Erkenntnislehre (Lucerne, 1892)
    Ontologie (Lucerne, 1896)
    La finalité (1899)

Vincent Knauer [T]
    Psychologie (Vienna, 1885)

H. Koppehl [T]
    Die lehre vom Bösen (Jena, 1892)

Dr. Kranich [T]
    Die übernatürlichen Ordnung (Paderborn)

Kuhn [T]
    Glauben und Wissen (1860)

H. Langen [T]
    Von der Möglichkeit einer ewigen Weltschöpfung
        (1864-65)

F. X. Leitner [T]
    Das unfehlbare Lehramt des Papstes
        (Freiburg i. B., 1872)
    Das unfehlbare Lehramt der Kirche
        (Regensburg, 1874)

J. A. Manser [T]
    Possibilitas praemotionis
        (Friburg, Switz., 1896)

Max Maurenbrecher [T]
    Das Wirthschaftsleben (Leipzig, 1898)

Joseph Mausbach [T]
    De voluntate (Paderborn, 1888)
    Der Begriff des sittlich Guten (Fribourg, 1897)
    Thomas von Aquin (Freiburg i. B., 1899)

Merx [T]
   Wie verstand Thomas "super hanc petram" (1879)

D. Mettenleiter [T W5]
   Geschichte des hl. Thomas (Regensburg, 1856)

Mittermüller [T]
   Die Benediktineruniversität Salzburg (1884)

W. Molsdorf [T]
   Die Idee des Schönen (Jena, 1891)

Francis Mortgott (d. 1900) [A T]
   Geist und Natur (Eichstatt, 1860)
   Die Theorie des Gefühle (Eichstatt, 1864)
   Die Mariologie (Freiburg, 1878)

A. Neander [T]
   Die Eintheilung der Tugenden (1846)

E. Neumayr [T]
   Theorie des Strebens (Bozen, 1888)

J. N. P. Oischinger [T]
   Die spekulative Theologie (Landshut, 1858)

A. Otten [T]
   Erkenntnislehre (Paderborn, 1882)

F. S. Petz [T]
   Kosmos und Psyche (Mainz, 1879)

Francis Xavier Pfeifer (1829-1902) [S6 T T2]
   St. Thomas und Aeterni Patris (Augsburg, 1881)
   Die Einheit der Seele (1889)

Herman Ernest Plassmann (1817-64) [H T W5]
   Die Schule des hl. Thomas (Paderborn, 1857-72)
   Die Moral (Soest, 1861)

A. Portmann [T]
   Das System der theologischen Summae
     (Lucerne, 1885)
   Quaestiones disputatae (1891-93)
   De regimine principum (Lucerne, 1897)

L. Rabus [T]
    Zur Philosophie des Thomas (1890)

Regler [T]
    Die sieben Gaben (Regensburg, 1899)

G. Reinhold [T]
    Die Eucharistie (Vienna, 1893)

A. Rietier [T]
    Die Moral (Munich, 1858)

A. Ritschl [T]
    Drei akademische Reden (Bonn, 1887)

A. Rittler [T]
    Wesenheit und Dasein (1887)

Eugene Rolfes [T]
    Die Gottesbeweise (Cologne, 1898)

H. Ruland [T]
    Compendium theologiae (Paderborn, 1863)

J. Sachs [T]
    Metaphysik (Paderborn, 1896)

Francis Schaub [S6 T]
    Die Eigenthumslehre (Freiburg i. B., 1898)

Matthias Joseph Scheeben (1835-88) [M2 T]
    The Mysteries of Christianity (St. Louis, 1951)

Th. Scherrer-Bonard [T]
    De regimine principum (Lucerne, 1897)

S. Schindele [T]
    Wesenheit und Dasein (Munich, 1900)

Fr. Seraph Schmeitzl [T]
    Erkenntnislehre (Munich, 1861)

Mathias Schneid (1840-95) [A T T2 W5]
    Die Philosophie (Wurzburg, 1881)
    Die Neuere thomistische Litteratur
        (Muenster, 1881)
    Die Psychologie (Paderborn, 1892)

Louis Schütz (1838-1901) [T T2]
   Die Lehre des Thomas (1877)
   Thomas Lexicon (Paderborn, 1881)
   Die vis aestimativa (Cologne, 1884)

E. Siegfried [T]
   Thomas als Ausleger des Alten Testaments (1894)

Julius Stahl [F]

Albert Stöckl (1825-95) [H T2 W5]
   Lehrbuch der Philosophie (Mainz, 1868)
   Die thomistiche Lehre (Mainz, 1883)

N. Thoemes [T W5]
   De republica christiana (Berlin, 1875)

H. Thüring [T]
   Die Willensfreiheit (1891)

W. Többe [T]
   Die Gottes-Mutter (Muenster, 1892)

H. Vandenesch [T]
   De concupiscentia (Bonn, 1871)

G. von Hertling [T]
   De spiritualibus creaturis (1884)

Emanuel von Ketteler [T W5]
   Die Pflichten des Adels (Mainz, 1868)

Constantine von Schaezler (d. 1880) [H W5]
   Das Dogma von der Menschwerdung Gottes
      (Freiburg i. B., 1870)
   Divus Thomas (Rome, 1874)

Al. von Schmid [T]
   Die Seinsweise Gottes (Fribourg, 1897)

Francis von Tessen Wesierski [T]
   Die Grundlagen des Wunderbegriffes
      (Paderborn, 1899)

Wangenmann [T]
   Thomas von Aquino (1885)

Charles Weiss [T]
    De satisfactione (published)
    Der Begriff der Tugend (1893)
    De donis Spiritus Sancti (Vienna, 1895)

Charles Werner (1821-88) [T W2]
    Der hl. Thomas (Regensburg, 1858-59)
    Die Kosmologie (Vienna, 1873)

I. Wild [T]
    Das Mass der Nützlichkeit (published)

                    Great Britain

A. J. Carlyle [T]
    Political Theories (1896)

R. W. Carlyle [T]
    Church and State (1896)

Th. Davidson [T]
    Revival of Philosophy (1882)
    Work of St. Thomas (1883)

R. D. Hampden [T]
    Life of St. Thomas (London, 1848)
    Scholastic Philosophy (Hereford, 1848)

Francis F. C. Hays [T]
    St. Thomas (London, 1889)

William Humphrey [T]
    The Sacraments (London, 1867)
    The Incarnation (London, 1868)

R. B. Vaughan [T]
    The Life and Labours of St. Thomas
        (London, 1872)

Walker [T]
    The origin of Knowledge (London, 1858)

                    Holland

F. Becker [T]
    Le principe de causalité (Amiens, 1877)

B. Bruin [T]
  Socialisme (1899)

J. M. L. Keuller [T]
  Sint Thomas (1897)

G. H. Lauers [T]
  Thomas van Aquin (Utrecht, 1896)

Will. Huh. Nolens [T]
  Over het recht (Utrecht, 1890)

H. J. A. M. Schaepmann [T]
  St. Thomas (Utrecht, 1898)

Constant Suermondt [A]
  Worked on the Leonine edition of Aquinas's
    works

H. Szalay [T]
  De geestelijkeid der menschelijke ziel (1897)

Vanes [T]
  Pius IX over den hl. Thomas (Utrecht, 1872)

                    Hungary

John Kiss [S6]

J. Kozáry [S6]

J. Ochaba [S6]

Ottokarus Prohászka [S6]
  God and the World (1891)
  Heaven and Earth (1901)

St. Székely [S6]
  Instinct and Intellect (1898)

L. Szilvek [S6]
  Physics and Metaphysics (Pécs, 1894)

                    Italy

Francis Acri (1834-1913) [C]
  S. Tommaso e Aristotele (Bologna, 1908)

Cerboni all´Albertini [C P P7]

R. Aloisio [T]
    Opuscoli inediti (Naples, 1890)

Aug. Angelini [T]
    Obiezioni, istanze, ed accuse (1883)
    In difesa di S. Tommaso (1883)

Maximilian Anselmi (1819-87) [D D2 H]
    Utrum bonum fuerit adhibere S. Thomam in schola
        metaphysice
    Tractatus de Deo
    Ethica
    De cognitione qua anima cognoscit seipsam

Giacomo Arbois [T]
    Saggio di fisica e chemica (Paris, 1880)

J. Astromoff [T]
    Ad intelligendam doctrinam Angelici
        (Rome, 1884)

William Audisio [P W5]

Vincent Bacchi [P]

Ferdinand Balsamo [R9]
    L´Unita cattolica (Cosenza, 1859)
    La dottrina cattolica (Cosenza, 1864)

F. Barba [T]
    S. Tommaso d´Aquino (1874-75)

A. Barone [T]
    San Tommaso (Nola, 1889)

Francis Battaglini (b. 1823) Cardinal [V W5]
    Logicae, metaphysicae, ethicae, institutiones
        (Bologna,1868)

Joseph Baviera [P]

R. Benzoni [T]
    La filosofia dell´Academia Romana (1886)

Joseph Berardinelli [T]
    Il papa e S. Tommaso (Bologna, 1880)

James Bernardi [T]
    S. Tommaso (Venice, 1880)

C. Bertani [T]
    Intorno alla passione (Milan, 1864)

Ermete Binzecher [P P5]
    La filosofia de Luigi Bonelli (Rome, 1875)

Alexander Biondi (d. 1874) [P]
    Iuris publici naturalis elementa (Rome, 1859)

Oreste Bodoyra [T]
    Della vera libertà (Turin, 1874)

Charles Bonacinna [T]
    Sul concorso generale di Dio (Milan, 1889)

S. Bonaldo [T]
    Maestro di giusto governo (1880)

Christopher Bonavino (pseudonym Ausonio Franchi)
(1821-95) [D2 P T]
    Sulla teoria del giudizio (Milan, 1870)
    S. Thomas (1887)
    Ultima critica (Milan, 1889-93)

John Bonetti [T]
    Compendio della vita (Turin, 1893)

A. M. Bonito [T]
    La Chiesa (Naples, 1881)

Henry Borgianelli [T]
    Il soprannaturale (Naples, 1891)

Vincent Brancia (d. 1896) [R9]
    La verità (Reggio Emilia, 1873)

Ignatius Joseph Brighenti [T]
    Orazione (Venice, 1853)

G. Bucceroni [T]
    Theologia moralis (Rome, 1893)

Gen. Bucchi [T]
    L´amore (Pistoia, 1887)
    Le passioni (Florence, 1888)

Ant. Burri [T]
    Le teorie politiche (Rome, 1884)

Joseph Buscarini (1819-72) [V W5]
    Discussioni di filosofia razionale (1856)
    Dialoghi politico-filosofici
    Discussioni de antropologia

Vincent Buzzetti (1777-1824) Canon [R]
    Institutiones philosophicae (Piacenza, 1940-41)
    Confutazione di Giovanni Locke
    Confutazione dell´idealismo di Condillac

Ignatius John Cadolini (1794-1850) [C]

Salvatore Calvanese [F P5 T]
    Del sistema nella storia naturale
        (Naples, 1864)
    Della conoscenza sensitiva (1893)

Hadrian Camanzi (1853-99) [C]
    S. Tommaso d´Aquino
    Scetticismo

Caneva [R8]

E. Cano [T]
    Orazione panegirica (Bosa, 1879)

A. Capelli [T]
    S. Tommaso e Dante (Naples, 1874)

F. Capello [T]
    Principii de filosofia (1890)

Andrew Cappellazzi (1854-1932) [B3 T]
    La conoscenza che Dio ha delle cose
        (Parma, 1893)
    La persona (Siena, 1899)
    La schiavitù (Crema, 1900)

B. Cappuccini [T]
    La scolastica (Camerino, 1892)

Philip Capri [R9]
   Saggio di filosofia fondamentale
      (Reggio Calabria, 1872)

Joseph Caproni [P T]
   Sul rinnovamento della filosofia (Pisa, 1874)

Louis Caranzetti [P]

Aliminda Cardinal [P]

Dom. Cargiulo [T]
   Sermones (Naples, 1846)

I. Carini [T]
   S. Tommaso e la Sicilia (Palermo)

Raphael Carnevali [T]
   Vita di S. Tommaso (Foligno, 1882)

D. Casalini [T]
   S. Tommaso e Dante (1885)

Francis Cassano [R9]
   Considerazioni filosofiche (Cosenza, 1875)

D. Castaseyna [T]
   Panegirico (Genoa, 1898)

C. Castelletti [T]
   La scienza moderna (Bergamo, 1881)

S. Castellote [T]
   La fisica razionale (1884)

L. Cattorini [T]
   La percezione intellettiva (1885)

Salvatore Cavalrese [T]
   La sistema nella storia naturale (Naples, 1884)

M. Celesia [T]
   Il secolo di S. Tommaso (Palermo, 1874)

F. Cerruti [T]
   Principii pedagogico-sociali (Turin, 1893)

Peter Chiaf [B3]

Chiaffi [W5]

Louis Coletta [T]
    S. Tommaso (1874)

Contini [T]
    Criterio tomistico (1878)

Raff. Coppola [T]
    S. Tommaso e le scienze (Milan, 1874)

Olindo Corsini [P]

Victor M. Costatini [P]

Clino Crosta [B3]

D. T. Cucchi [T]
    Circa Immaculatam Conceptionem (1882-86)

Titus M. Cucchi [T]
    De academia Romana thomistica (1893)

A. d´Aniello [T]
    De Aquinate (Naples, 1900)

Joseph d´Annibale (fl. 1884) Cardinal [P5]

E. de Caria [T]
    Philosophia (Naples, 1889)

V. de Crescenzo [T]
    Il problema degli universali (published)

A. de Giorgio [T W5]
    Institutiones philosophicae (Paris, 1854)

John Baptist De Giorgio [P]
    Institutiones philosophicae
        (2nd ed., Udine, 1865)

Vincent de Grazia [F W5]

M. de Jorio [T]
    Contra pantheismum Hegelii (Tiferni, 1887)

F. de Leo [O2 T]
    Creazione nella scienza (Naples, 1878)

G. della Cella [T]
   S. Tommaso all'Istituto di Francia (1893-94)

John della Valle [T]
   Dell'origine delle idee (Faenza, 1874)

John de Luca [T]
   Saggio ontologico (1870)
   Il misticismo cattolico (1874)

George De Lucchi [P]

G. de Luise [T]
   Catechetica (Naples, 1874)

G. de Mattia [T]
   L'origine dell'anima (Naples, 1900)

A. C. de Meis [T]
   De mente et doctrina Thomae (Macerata, 1880)

P. de Nardi [T]
   I nuovi tomisti (1890)
   Tommaso d'Aquino (Forli, 1898)

P. d'Ercole [T]
   Il teismo (Turin, 1884)

Sante de Sanctis [T]
   La vera sapienza (Bari, 1874)

Silvester di San Giovanni Evangelista [W5]

G. Doria [T]
   La filosofia (Tortona, 1879)

John Gr. Dorscheus [T]
   La origine del potere (1849)
   La Eucharistia (1891-92)

F. D'Orsi [02 T]
   Personalità (1876)

A. Doublet [T]
   Gesù Cristo (Turin, 1898)

F. Durso [T]
   La razione umana (Bologna, 1874)

John Fabri [P5 T]
    Utrum intellectus sit potentia passiva (1882)
    Le specie intelligibili (1884)
    Utrum anima seipsam cognoscat (1886)

P. Faggioli [T]
    Conoscenza umana (Faenza, 1880)

R. Fava [T]
    La morale (Naples, 1867)

P. M. Ferre [T]
    St. Thomas (London, 1875)
    Degli universali (Casale, 1880-86)

John Mary Mastai Ferretti (1792-1878) Pope Pius IX
[P P5]
    Tuas libenter (1863)
    Epistolae (June 11, 1852; May 2, 1874)

L. Ferri [T]
    L'academia Romana di S. Tommaso (1880)

L. C. Fietta [T]
    Della politica di San Tommaso (Venice, 1874)

E. Filippini [T]
    Tommaso d'Aquino (Rome, 1896)

G. Filoni [T]
    Scienza cristiana (Florence, 1876)

Alf. Fisichella [T]
    San Tommaso e la scienza (Catania, 1880)

Ernest Fontana [B3 P5 T]
    Utrum intellectus sit potentia animae (1883)
    Utrum intellectus intelligat res materiales
        (1885)
    Utrum anima possit intelligere substantias
        immateriales (1886)

L. Fossati [T]
    Psicologia tomistica (published)

E. Frai [T]
    La Immocolata Concezione (Sorrento, 1889)

Louis Francardi [T]
    Logica (1855)

Anthony Mary Franchini (1810-85) [C]

S. Frati [T]
   La composizione delle creature (Milan, 1887)

V. Gabrielli [T]
   Santo Tommaso (Rome, 1881)

E. Gaggio [T]
   Panegirico (Venice, 1893)

F. Gambardella [02 T]
   Santo Tommaso (Naples, 1877)

B. Gargiulo [T]
   Il Tasso (Naples, 1895)
   Del sistema scientifico di San Tommaso
      (Sansevero, 1898)

Gastaldi [T]
   Nel sesto centenario (Turin, 1874)
   St. Thomas (Turin, 1883)

Geny [F]

J.-Th. Ghilardi [T]
   Sermones quadragesimales (Monreale, 1872)

Giacomo of the Sacred Heart of Mary [T]
   L'azione de Dio (Naples, 1877)

V. Gibelli [T]
   Vita di S. Tommaso (Bologna, 1855)

Louis Giordano [T]
   Lectiones logicae et metaphysicae
      (Vigevano, 1881)
   Circa psychologicam idearum originem
      (Vigevano, 1881)

Ferdinand Giovannucci [P P6]
   Opere teologiche

F. Giovanzana [T]
   Un punto capitalissimo (Bergamo, 1885)

Philip Giriodi [R R8]
   De religione

G. Giustiniani [T]
   Omaggio alla Madre di Dio (Naples, 1875)

F. Granato [T]
   Ateismo (Naples, 1877)

B. Granta [O2]
   Dell´ideale della virtu (c. 1875)

Louis James Grassi [T]
   S. Tommaso (Genoa, 1888)

Joseph M. Graziosi (d. 1847) [P P5 P6]
   Logicae et metaphysicae institutiones
   Logicae et metaphysicae theses

Gir. Guadagnin [T]
   Della umana felicità (Treviso, 1882)
   Sul libro di Boezio (Treviso, 1882)

A. Gualandi [T]
   Summa theologica (Rome, 1881)

L. Gualandi [T]
   Tre questioni importantissime (Rome, 1887)

Louis Lauda [T]
   S. Tommaso (Benevento, 1881)

Joseph Lemius [H]

V. Lilla [T]
   La mente dell´Aquinate (Turin, 1873)

Cajetan Livezzani Cirelli (1821-82) [C]
   Articles in Il Populo (Ferrara)

Joseph lo Bue [T]
   Elogio (Palermo, 1841)

A. Lombardo [T]
   Della conoscenza (Milan, 1858)

Benedict Lorenzelli (1853-1915) [F H P5 S6 T]
   De intellectu humano (1886)
   Philosopiae theoreticae institutiones
      (Rome, 1890)

P. Lucio [T]
    Supremum veritatis criterium (Prato, 1884-85)

G. P. Maffei [T]
    Vita di S. Tommaso (Rome, 1842)

F. Magani [T]
    La grandezze della Madonna (Pavia, 1882)

Salvatore Magnasco (1806-92) [P]
    Institutiones theologiae dogmatico-scholasticae
        (Genoa, 1976-80)

Mamachi [P]

Dominic Mannaioli [P]
    De officio adherendi germanae Doctoris Angelici
        philosophiae (Rome, 1914)

L. Manzoni [T]
    La civilta europea, tr. (Naples, 1882)

Marchetti [T]
    Filosofia moderna (1878)

I. Marchini [T]
    Cenni storici dell'Angelico (Genoa, 1875)

Anthony Marini [T]
    Il centenario di S. Tommaso (1873-74)

Marotta d'Aquino [T]
    Omaggio storico a S. Tommaso (1874)

L. Martani [T]
    Lo studio della filosofia tomistica
        (Piacenza, 1889)

L. Mascheroni [T]
    In lode di S. Tommaso (Naples, 1868)

A. Masinelli [T]
    La filosofia (1882)

Masini [W5]

M. Menichini [T]
    Del vero, del buono, e del bello (1879)
    San Tommaso e Dante (1887)
    La storia naturale (published)

Peter Merighi (1820-1906) [C]
    Idealismo e positivismo (Bologna, 1898)
    Philosophia rationalis

G. Milanese [T]
    Nella fiesta di S. Tommaso (Treviso, 1887)

Dalmazio Minoretti (Cardinal) [B3]

Al. Missaglia [M2]
    Summula D. Thomae (Rome, 1899)

A. Moglia [T]
    La filosofia di S. Tommaso (Piacenza, 1885)

Peter Montagnani (1843-1902) [V]
    Rosmini, S. Tommaso, e la logica
        (Bologna, 1888-89)
    Tomisti e Neotomisti (Rome, 1891)

Thomas Mora [T]
    Discorso in lode (Vercelli, 1876)

Peter Morassi [T]
    Orazione all'Angelico (Parma, 1869)

Bonfiglio Mura (Servite) (fl. 1852) [P5]

P. Naddeo [T]
    Il pensiero filosofico (1890)

Louis Nicora [B3]

E. M. Nurra [T]
    Del Immaculato Concepimento (1853)

Sebastian Olivieri [T]
    De ideologia (Genoa, 1890)

G. Olmi [T]
    Sul ss. Sacramento (Genoa, 1881)

G. Papa [O2]
    Ragionando di S. Tommaso (c. 1875)

Lucido Mary Parocchi (1833-1903) Cardinal [P5 P6]
    S. Tommaso (Padua, 1874)
    Della necessità di una filosofia
       (Bologna, 1877)

Pastrizio a Liberio di Gesù [P P7]

Joachim Pecci (1810-1903) Pope Leo XIII [H]
    Aeterni Patris (Vatican City, 1879)
    Iampridem considerando (Vatican City, 1879)
    Cum hoc sit (1880)
    De Sancto Thoma Aquinate (1880)

Joseph Pecci (1807-90) Cardinal [H T]
    Comm. De ente (Rome, 1882)
    Studi sulla Psicologia

M. A. Pedrotti [T]
    Umano sapere (1885)

Gioacchino Pelagatti (1840-1902) [P T]
    S. Tommaso (Siena, 1886)
    Compendio di teologia, Opuscoli di S. Tommaso
       (Florence, 1894)

Augustine Peruzzi (1764-1850) [C]
    Opere (Bologna, 1844-46)

F. Petronius [T]
    Comm. SCG (Naples, 1886)

Placido Pigliacelli [P6]

John Pindemonte [T]
    Oraziione (Verona, 1809)

Giac. Poletto [T]
    Libertà e lege (Padua, 1883)
    Dizionario dantesco (Siena and Verona, 1885-87)

Gennaro Portanova (fl. 1878) [H O2 P5]
    Errori e deliri del Darwinismo (Naples, 1872)

Joseph Prisco (1833-1923) [H P5 T T2]
    La metafisica della morale (Naples, 1865)
    Principii di filosofia del diritto
       (Naples, 1872)

R. Puccini [T]
   La teorica del numero infinito (Fribourg, 1898)

Peter Ragnisco [T]
   Della fortuna di S. Tommaso (Padua, 1892)

C. Ramellini [T]
   De intelligere Dei (1894-96)
   Comm. III (1897)

Anthony Ranza [P R8]

G. Raynaud [T]
   Teologia scolastica (Naples, 1857)

Thomas Reggio [P]

A. Riboldi [T]
   La fisica di San Tommaso (published)

Peter Aloysius Rispoli (Redemptorist) [T]
   Lux praedicatorum (Naples, 1815)

B. Roetti [T]
   La ss. Eucaristia (Turin)

Cajetan Roncato [T]
   Orazione (Padua, 1894)

Caesar Roncetti [P6]

John Baptist Rossi [T]
   Nel sesto centenario (Bologna, 1874)
   Sulla dottrina di S. Tommaso (Concordia, 1886)

C. Rossini [T]
   Dizionario (Naples, 1856)

Louis Rotelli (1833-91) Cardinal [H T]
   Comm. I (1888-91)
   Comm. III (1893-96)

Emidio Ruggieri [P5]
   Dell'antica filosofia (Rome, 1881)

Frederick Sala [B3]

Henry Sala [B3]

L. Salvatorelli [T]
    Santo Tommaso interprete della S. Scrittura
        (1878)

Cajetan Sanseverino (1811-65) [H T]
    I principali sistemi della filosofia
        (Naples, 1853)
    La dottrina di S. Tommaso (Naples, 1853)
    Philosophia christiana (Naples, 1853)
    Institutiones philosophicae
        (Vatican City, 1974)

Vincent Santi (d. 1892) [H T]
    San Tommaso e lo spiritualismo (Perugia, 1890)

V. Sarnelli [02]
    Le relazioni fra la Chiesa e lo Strato
        (c. 1875)

Francis Satolli (1839-1910) Cardinal [H M2 S6 T]
    Comm. ST (Rome, 1887)
    De habitibus (Rome, 1897)

John Baptist Scalabrini [P]

P. M. Scarpati [T]
    Antropologia (Naples, 1890)

Lawrence Schiavi [P5 T W5]
    Logica (Padua, 1898)

L. Schioppa [T]
    La psicologia (Naples, 1895)

John Baptist Scolari [T]
    L'Impero e il Papato (Sessa, 1870)

J. Semeria [T]
    Actus fidei (Piacenza, 1891)

Joachim Sestili [T]
    De appetitu intuendi divinam essentiam
        (Naples and Rome, 1896)

Mgr. Giacomo Sichirollo [T]
    La mia conversione da Rosmini a S. Tommaso
        (Padua, 1882)

Nunzio Signoriello (1821-89) [D2 F T]
    Lexicon Peripateticum (Naples, 1893)
    Compendio della filosofia cristiana
        (Naples, 1894)

B. Sorio [T]
    S. Paolo ai Galati (Verona, 1862)

T. M. Straniero [T]
    La vita di S. Tommaso (Venice, 1885)

R. Tabarelli (Stimmatine) (d. 1909) [F P5]
    L´argomento ontologico (Parma, 1887)
    De Deo uno (Rome, 1904)

Joseph Taddei (1806-75) [C]
    Specimen casuum conscientiae (Ferrara, 1870)

Salvatore Talamo (1854-1932) [H S6 T]
    Il rinnovamento del pensiero tomistico
        (Siena, 1878)
    L´odierna scuola tomistica (Siena, 1879)
    Il concetto della schiavitù (Rome, 1881)

Tamba [W5]

Peter Tarino (1852-99) [V W5]
    Istituzioni de logica e metafisica
        (Biella, 1862)
    Istituzioni de filosofia morale (Biella, 1863)
    Institutiones philosophicae (Biella, 1863-64)

Angelo Testa [R R8]
    Institutiones philosophicae

N. Tommaseo [T]
    I santi evangeli (Milan, 1886)

J. B. Tornatore [T]
    De cognitionis modo (Piacenza, 1885)
    De natura rei materialis et immaterialis
        (Piacenza, 1887)
    De ente communi (1890)

Alphonse Travaglini [H]

Hyacinth Tredici [B3]

Peter Anthony Uccelli (d. 1880) [B3 P T W5]
    SCG (Paris, 1858)
    Memorie del sexto centenario (1874-77)
    Opuscula (Rome, 1881)

G. Vadala-Papale [T]
    Le leggi (Catania, 1894)

Anthony Valdameri [B3]

Dominic Valensise (1832-1916) [R9 T]
    Dell´idea (Naples, 1874)
    Dell´estetica (Reggio Emilia, 1877)
    De probabilitate (Piacenza, 1885)
    De bono (1894-96)
    De resurrectione (Newcastle, 1900)

G. Vanzolini [T]
    Somma delle penitenze (1873-74)

Joseph Vercillo (1792-1864) [R9]
    Osservazioni
    La Madre di Dio

Alphonse M. Vespignani (1825-1904) [T V]
    Saggio della teorica degli universali
        (Imola, 1860-67)
    Discorso inaugurale (1880)
    Sulla scetticismo (Imola, 1885)
    Della materia prima (Bologna, 1887)
    Dell´intelletto agente e dell´intelletto
        possibile (Parma, 1892)

A. Videmari [T]
    La poesia e le scienze positive (Turin, 1888)

J. Vinati [T]
    De relatione (1890-91)

A. Zacchi [F]

G. Zanon [T]
    La luce corporale (1884)

Emmanuel Zorzoli [B3]

P. Zurla [T]
    Enchiridion (Verona, 1861)

Malta

A. Galea [T]
    De opusculis Thomae (Malta, 1880)

Louis Galea [T]
    Comm. I (Malta, 1881)
    De charitate (Turin, 1895)

L. F. D. Pace [T]
    Lezioni di S. Scrittura (Malta, 1878)

Mexico

Segundino Briceño [S6 T2]
    La Filosofía de Spencer (Léon, 1894)

Rafael Cagigas (1864-90) [S6 T2]
    Obras (Mexico, 1890)

Saint Anthony Mary Claret (Claretian) (d. 1870)
[W5]

Augustine de la Rosa (b. 1824) [S6 T2]
    La Verdad (Guadalajara, 1870)

J. M. Diez de Sollano y Davalos (1820-81) [S6 T T2]
    Logicae compendium (Léon, 1868)
    Carta pastoral (Léon, 1879)
    Obras completas (Mexico, 1894)

Nicanor Lozada [S6 T2]
    Filosofía católica (Mexico, 1880)

Melchor of Talamantes [G4]

Clement of Jesus Mungría [G4]

Joseph M. de Jesús Portugal [S6 T2]
   El Amable Jesús (Mexico, 1897)

Emeteris Valverde y Tellez [G4 S6 T2]
   La Verdad (Mexico, 1897)

Augustine F. Villa [S6 T2]
   Términos Escolásticos (Guadalajara, 1897)

Portugal

Bernard Augusto de Madureira [T2]
   Compendio de philosophia (Coimbra, 1896)

O. Ferreira-Deusdado [T]
   Eusino da philosofia thomista (1896)
   La philosophie thomiste en Portugal (1899)

Manuel Joseph Martins Capella [F3 S6 T2]
   L´opportunité de la philosophie thomiste
      (Braga, 1892)

Francis de Paule Peixoto da Silva et Bourbon
(b. 1868?) [F3]
   Le Créateur, l´Homme, et la Nature
      (Coimbra, 1887)

Clement Pereira Gomez de Carvalho [F3 T2]
   Elementos de philosophia (Coimbra, 1894)

Tiago Sinibaldi [F3 T]
   Praelectiones philosophiae (Coimbra, 1889)
   Sistema fisico (1891)

Joseph Soriano de Sousa [F3 T2]
   Lecons de philosophie élémentaire
      (Pernambuco, 1871)

Teixera Guedes [F3 S6 T2]
   Conférence inaugurale (1897)

Scandinavia

R. Krogh-Tonning [T]
    De gratia Christi (Oslo, 1898)

N. J. Linnarson [T]
    Moral-theologie (Uppsala, 1866)

Spain

Giacomo Arlos [W5]

James Luciano Balmes (1810-48) [N T W2]
    El criterio (Barcelona, 1845)
    Filosofia fundamental (Barcelona, 1846)

Anthony Berjon y Vasquez [T]
    Las obras de Santo Tomás (Madrid, 1899)

F. Breva [T]
    Sermon (Valencia, 1804)

J. D. Cortes (1809-61) [W2]

Francis Cuadrato (Augustinian) [H3 T]
    De virtutibus (Madrid, 1877)

V. de la Fuente [T]
    La enseñanza tomistica en España (Madrid, 1874)

M. del Amo y Agreda [T]
    Elementos di psychologia, logica, e etica
        (Madrid, 1897)

F. Fernandez [T]
    Doctrinas juridicas (Madrid, 1889)

Anthony Hernandez y Fajarnés [T T2]
    Ontologia (1887)
    Cosmologia (1893)

Llorens [S6]

Raymond Marti de Eixala (d. 1857) [S6 T2]
    Curso de filosofía elemental (Barcelona, 1841)

R. Martinez Vigil [T]
    Discurso (Madrid, 1880)

J. Miralles y Sibert [T]
    El moderno regimen constitucional
        (Madrid, 1890)

Anthony Monescillo (1811-97) [W5]

C. Morata [T]
    Sermon de S. Tomás (Valencia, 1800)

John Emmanuel Orti y Lara (1826-1904) [T W2 W5]
    Metafisica (Madrid, 1887)
    Psicologia (Madrid, 1890)

Alexander Pidal y Mon (1846-1913) [T T2]
    Santo Tomás (Madrid, 1875)

M. Polo y Pyrolon [T]
    Elogio (Madrid, 1880)

A. J. Pou y Orderas [T]
    Los jurisconsultos (1887)

Narcisco Puig (d. 1865) [A S W2]
    Institutiones theologicae (1861-63)

T. Rodriquez [T]
    La Immaculada Concepcion (1885)

Salado y Morejon [T]
    Santo Tomás (Murcia, 1882)

M. Salvany [T]
    El concepto de Dios (1885)

Joseph Torras y Bages (fl. 1880) [E2]
    Fecit utraque unum

Francis Xarrié (d. 1866) [A S W2]
    Theologia thomistica

J. M. Zama Mellinio [T]
Vocabulario de terminos (Guadalajara, 1879)

United States and Canada

A. Bierbauer [T]
St. Thomas (1883)

Gennaro Louis Vincent de Concilio (b. 1835)
[S6 T T2]
    Elements of Intellectual Philosophy
        (New York, 1874)
    Catholicism and Pantheism (New York, 1881)
    On the Right of Property (New York, 1887)

A. P. Edward [T]
Modern Thought (1896)

John Gmeiner (1847-1913) [M S6 T W2]
    Modern Scientific Views (Milwaukee, 1884)
    Mediaeval and Modern Cosmology
        (Milwaukee, 1891)

Alexander MacDonald (b. 1858) [T T2]
    Evolution (1895-96)
    The Memory (1902)

Cornelius O'Brien (1843-1906) [S6]
    Philosophy of the Bible (1876)

E. A. Pace [M T]
    St. Thomas and Modern Thought (1896)
    The Soul (1898)
    Immortality (1900)

Louis A. Paquet [T T2]
    Disputationes theologicae (Quebec, 1893-1903)

William Turner [T2]
    Erigena and Aquinas (1897)

Unknown Country

J. H. Defouri [T]
St. Thomas Aquinas in Mexico (1882)

C. Hargrove [T]
    St. Thomas (1880)

S. S. Hebrard [T]
    The future life (1882)

Keesen [T]
    La mission de l'état (Brussels, 1890)

M. Snell [T]
    The Triumph of St. Thomas (1899)

Ignatius Torregrossa [T]
    De constitutione corporum (1894-95)

Walsch [T]
    Doctor gratiae (1898)

Index of Thomists

Because of the large size of this index it has not been possible to have more than one entry per person. A person is listed under his last name if he has one that can be called such. Most of the medievals are listed under their first name. In the long transitional period to modern practice, decisions as to listing have been made on an ad hoc basis. It is unfortunate also that there is such variety in the spelling of both first and last names, but one particular one had to be chosen. Please note, however, that most first names have been anglicized.

OTHER PUBLICATIONS OF

THE CENTER FOR THOMISTIC STUDIES

Thomistic Papers I
Victor B. Brezik, C.S.B., ed.

Thomistic Papers II
Leonard A. Kennedy, C.S.B.,
& Jack C. Marler, eds.

Thomistic Papers III
Leonard A. Kennedy, C.S.B., ed.

Wisdom from St. Augustine
Vernon J. Bourke

One Hundred Years of Thomism
Aeterni Patris and Afterwards:
A Symposium
Victor B. Brezik, C.S.B., editor

About Beauty:
A Thomistic Interpretation
Armand A. Maurer, C.S.B.

An Elementary Christian Metaphysics
Joseph Owens, C.Ss.R.

An Interpretation of Existence
Joseph Owens, C.Ss.R.

All publications of the Center are sold by:

University of Notre Dame Press
Notre Dame, Indiana 46556